Patrick Gwynne

TWENTIETH CENTURY ARCHITECTS

Patrick Gwynne

Neil Bingham

Published by Liverpool University Press on behalf of
Historic England, The Engine House, Fire Fly Avenue, Swindon SN2 2EH
www.HistoricEngland.org.uk

Historic England is a Government service championing England's heritage and giving expert, constructive advice.

© Neil Bingham 2023

The views expressed in this book are those of the author and not necessarily those of Historic England.

First published 2023
ISBN 978-1-80207-754-4 paperback

British Library Cataloguing in Publication data
A CIP catalogue record for this book is available from the British Library.

Neil Bingham has asserted the right to be identified as the author of this book in accordance with the Copyright, Designs and Patents Act 1988.

All rights reserved
No part of this publication may be reproduced or transmitted in any form or by any means, electronic or mechanical, including photocopying, recording, or any information storage or retrieval system, without permission in writing from the publisher.

Application for the reproduction of images should be made to Historic England. Every effort has been made to trace the copyright holders and we apologise in advance for any unintentional omissions, which we would be pleased to correct in any subsequent edition of this book.

Series editors: Timothy Brittain-Catlin, Barnabas Calder, Geraint Franklin, Elain Harwood and Alan Powers

Typeset in Quadraat, 10.75pt
Edited by Sarah Enticknap
Page layout by Carnegie Book Production
Printed in Wales by Gomer Press.

Front cover: The Homewood, Esher, Surrey, completed 1938
Frontispiece: Vista Point, Angmering-on-Sea, Sussex, completed 1970
Back cover: Patrick Gwynne at The Homewood, 1993

Contents

	Foreword by Alan Powers	vii
	Preface	xi
1	Early life: 1913–30	1
2	Becoming an architect: 1930–37	11
3	The Homewood: 1937–39	25
4	The war and mid-century modern: 1940–59	39
5	The art of living: 1960–84	73
6	The Homewood: 1940–2003	111
	Notes	125
	List of works	133
	Plans of houses and buildings	141
	Illustration credits	150
	Index	151

Foreword

The principal aim of the Twentieth Century Architects series, since the first titles appeared in 2009, has been to put in book form the work of architects who, for lack of a publication, have not received the attention they deserve. Patrick Gwynne was always uppermost in the minds of the editors, and Neil Bingham was always the obvious author, so the appearance of this work is a special occasion.

What makes Gwynne's architecture especially worthy of study? He belongs to a group of architects in post-war Britain who were committed to modernism, but in many ways belonged to an earlier time. Gwynne's small-scale, largely domestic practice would have seemed natural, for example, in the Arts and Crafts period. He valued his clients as friends and made distinctive houses for them that responded to their settings and to the sites. Like those precursors, he worked to resolve house plans that were full of incident and interest despite their small scale. His attention to interior details of surface and finish was in direct continuity with that earlier period, even if the aesthetic was different. It was different, too, to the dominant aesthetic of its period, with a baroque feeling for form and drama.

The basis of most of Gwynne's houses is not far removed from the Palladian villa, with a three-by-three grid, the central square being filled by a sinuous top-lit stair, an economical way of avoiding corridors. The walls often tuck themselves in with concave curves, giving the exterior a tailored body, or are rounded to avoid a box-like expression. On other occasions, the plan is Y-shaped, or angled like a boomerang. Here was an architect who enjoyed himself, unfettered by the restrictive puritanism common to modernism at the time. In some hands, the results might have been ill-judged or overdone, but having visited many of these houses, I believe he had a sure instinct for the nuances of expression.

Neil Bingham has touched on the issue of how far this body of work reflects Gwynne as a 'confirmed bachelor', in the euphemism of the time. This is significant partly because puritanism among the Moderns seems so often to have reflected a fear of visual pleasure and playfulness, and at times an outright homophobia. In 1950s Italy, his work would have been entirely

10 Blackheath Park, London, 1969

PATRICK GWYNNE

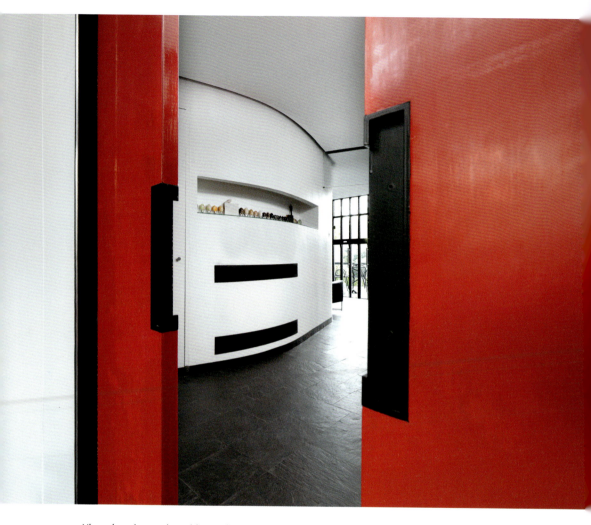

View along internal corridor to the garden deck, 10 Blackheath Park, London, completed in 1969

at home, but that in England it is exceptional adds to its interest and value. As John Potvin has written in *Bachelors of a Different Sort*, the domesticity of a range of men, whether in couples or not, constitutes 'a vital and yet decidedly neglected dimension of current scholarship on sexuality and design histories of the [post-war] period'.[1] Gwynne's houses, although largely commissioned by conventional households, provide evidence for just such an exploration into the poetics of a different sort of modernism.

While houses were in so many ways Gwynne's special area, his public work is full of interest. Who could have done a better version of the Dell Restaurant on the Serpentine in London – a form legible at a glance yet

FOREWORD

always a pleasure to see, enhancing a sensitive site. In York, the theatre foyer respects its Victorian parent through its difference, with a rigorous marriage of structure and geometry. How did Gwynne learn to design so well? His skill in arranging plans is phenomenal given their tiny scale, and yet the plain rectangle of the big room at his first project, The Homewood, Esher, is the boldest example in pre-war Britain of an open-plan space structured through light, surface finishes and the arrangement of furniture, so self-evident that its revolutionary character could go unnoticed.

One anecdote Patrick told me, but which seems otherwise unrecorded, is evidence of his profoundly architectural way of thinking. Denys [Lasdun] was designing the Royal College of Physicians, he explained, and sitting up late, drinking whisky and worrying about the design. Lasdun liked having Patrick round for company, and it was Patrick who suggested that the scheme would work better if it were rotated through 90 degrees so that the narrow end faced Regent's Park. The rightly praised result is there for all to see.

Designing The Homewood for his parents was Gwynne's lucky break. He repaid that luck by his devotion to the house and its garden, and his success in arranging its gifting to the National Trust in the last decade of his life, not without obstacles. Ernö Goldfinger's 2 Willow Road was the first modern classic to be added to that distinguished collection of domestic design and, as far back as 1945, The Homewood was the only other example of a prime modern house to have survived without the interruption of a change of ownership and clearance of the contents. They are a perfect pair – one example in town, and another in the country, each a complex, intriguing design with a dreamlike quality far removed from that tired cliché 'a machine for living in', and closer to what Le Corbusier added to that phrase to explain his real meaning: 'le lieu utile pour la meditation' – a useful place for meditation.[2]

ALAN POWERS

Preface

Patrick Gwynne's passing in 2003 received wide coverage, largely as a result of the gift of his own house, The Homewood, near Esher in Surrey, to the National Trust for England and Wales. The quality newspapers published extensive obituaries, and the major British architectural periodicals followed suit.[1] Since the subsequent opening of the house to the public, Gwynne's reputation and his architecture have found a new and growing audience. His work spans an astonishingly long period in modern architectural history, from the mid-1930s to the beginning of the present century.

Gwynne was the architect of innovative restaurants, shops, flats and, most notably, a collection of bespoke houses each as exquisitely tailor-made as a Savile Row suit. His houses, with interiors that brought comfort and pleasure, broke with the cool theoretical expressions of received architecture, as Alan Powers touches upon in the Foreword.[2] The purist attitude of the old hard-liners has given way, as mid-century modern design, so stylishly developed and executed by Gwynne, has become part of mainstream fashion. Likewise, renewed interest in Brutalism – architecture of raw surfaces, heavy forms and modularity – means that Gwynne's larger works of the 1960s and 1970s, like the York Theatre Royal, can be appreciated for a playfulness not often associated with the style.

Although The Homewood remains in the best of hands, many of Gwynne's works have suffered. Some have been demolished, most notably the Serpentine Restaurant and Grovewood and Ananda houses, and there have been inevitable alterations to most of his buildings as new owners come and go. House interiors are especially vulnerable; even after a building has been listed, its internal preservation is not necessarily secured.

There was also the tragic loss of some of Gwynne's archive material and furniture stored by the National Trust in the attic of Clandon Park, Surrey, when the house was destroyed by fire in 2015. The irony is that the retention of some of the original furniture at The Homewood had been deemed a legal fire risk, and had been replaced by replica pieces, which in a few cases were without Gwynne's details – such as the cleverly hidden cine-screen incorporated into the living room sofa. Other Gwynne purchases disappeared in the

The Firs, Spaniards End, London, 1959

fire, like the Bruno Mathsson chaise longue with its bespoke beaver-wool covering.[3] Uncannily, nine years earlier, in 2006, after news emerged that that some of The Homewood furniture was to be stored, the front page of *Building Design* had trumpeted 'Modern Furniture Banished from Gwynne's Homewood'.[4]

Gwynne and I met in May 1990, when I was deputy curator at the Royal Institute of British Architects (RIBA) Drawings Collection and with curator Jill Lever visited him to talk about his drawings coming into the collection. He picked us up at Esher train station. Arrival at The Homewood was a revelation, although my eye was not yet fully attuned to its many nuances. Only when I had returned to pick up the drawings and a model of Leslie Bilsby's courtyard house, and to interview Gwynne to aid their cataloguing, did I begin to appreciate fully the depth and breadth of the house, and his life and architecture. I was soon dropping around with friends, including Lady Gibberd who first suggested to him that he approach the National Trust. I took my parents and my sister Lynne, but usually I just went on my own, often to take more notes for articles and lectures. We also enjoyed many days out visiting his houses, most memorably to see Lady Brown at Witley Park. One evening I stayed overnight at The Homewood and Gwynne set up his movie projector to show his cinefilms, including one of his visit to the 1958 Brussels World's Fair. Our biggest endeavour together was six hours of interviews for National Life Stories. These recordings, available online, enable anyone to hear Gwynne speak of his life and work. They also have been invaluable for this book, allowing me to quote Patrick freely.[5]

Gwynne and his architecture should be viewed with an understanding of his sexuality because it unlocks further insights into his life and work. Being myself an openly gay man, I sometimes took my partner to see him, as well as gay friends and colleagues, but even with this familiarity, he never verbally expressed his own homosexuality to us or to any of his family. For men of his generation, this was a highly sensitive issue, and prior to the partial legalisation in Britain of homosexuality in 1967, by which time Gwynne was in his fifties, there existed an ever-present atmosphere of fear and oppression. Such state and societal persecutions define a person's life, guide decisions and steer relationships.

Gwynne was never given to architectural theory and had nothing published under his name. But his words and phrases can be read in the many journal and magazine articles covering his work, lifted by the writers from his press releases. Given the chance, he also styled his interiors for the photographs, arranging kitchenware, table settings and flowers to give his architecture an intimate and comfortable atmosphere, rare in architectural photography.

PREFACE

Patrick Gwynne with the author in the study at The Homewood, 1994

Besides the notes taken from our conversations and letters, I have been able to draw upon the captions and descriptions in the five albums of photographs that Gwynne compiled. Although these were lost in the Clandon Park fire, they had been scanned by the National Trust. From these albums, he self-published two slim plastic-ringed brochures of projects which he gave to clients and those interested in his work.[6] Also of use have been the transcribed conversations made by the Trust between their staff and Gwynne, mainly about The Homewood's history, construction and contents. For the Trust too, he produced thick reports on the house and garden.[7] Then there are his architectural drawings in the RIBA, an extensive collection but one that, like certain other parts of his life story, Gwynne heavily weeded. The RIBA also holds a great number of photographs of his work among the archives of many of the distinguished architectural photographers of his period.

Past clients and friends of Gwynne have been invaluable in sharing their memories. Raymond and Janet Menzies were his closest friends and, with their children, his second family; I owe them my deepest gratitude. In Gwynne's own family, his nephew George Cruddas especially has been a great support. John Allan and Fiona Lamb of Avanti Architects kindly

xiii

shared their work on The Homewood. David Scott and Louise Cavanagh, the present residents of The Homewood, assisted enthusiastically. And my special thanks go to my friends and colleagues Alan Powers, Elain Harwood, Timothy Brittain-Catlin and Catherine Croft of the Twentieth Century Society who have been so helpful and patient with me in getting this book written and published. Also, I would like to thank Historic England, especially James O Davies for his fine architectural photography of Gwynne's buildings. We are most grateful for the sponsorship of William Sargent, Raymond Menzies, David Scott, Oliver Richards, George Cruddas and the Marc Fitch Fund.

Others I wish to thank are Helena Appio, Elvine (Cottrell) Baird, Lady Brown, Anne Bruh, Sophie Chesham, Elizabeth Darling, Edward Diestelkamp, Neil Einarson, Alistair Fair, Robin Fawcett, Bill Finch, Susie Gerhartz, Vivien Griffiths, Dirk van den Heuvel, Sarah Howard, Tanya House, Sarah Howard, Jon Howell and Clare Swinson, Jonathan Hoyle, Bernard Jay, Robert (Bob) King, Tim Knox, Fiona Lamb, William Lasdun, David Lawrence, David Lingard, Stefan Menzies and Tina Gordan, Fiona Orsini, Luis Peral Aranda, Henry Phythian-Adams, Oliver Richards, Anthony Salmon, Robert Sempijja, Joanne Shaw, Paulene Stone, Ana Sutherland, Jenny Shanahan, Lucy Shanahan, Susan and Peter Taylor, Wolfgang Voigt. And to the National Trust and RIBA, I am most grateful.

The architect Sir Hugh Casson said of the fabulously wealthy Stanley J Seeger that he regarded 'the chic as a badge of insecurity and the conventional as a signal of surrender'.[8] Is it little wonder that Seeger chose Gwynne as his architect?

PREFACE

The living room of The Homewood, photographed in 1993 by Mark Fiennes

1 Early life 1913–30

Months before Christmas, Patrick Gwynne would flip to the most treasured page in his ring-bound recipe book. On an old piece of pink-ruled paper, annotated by Gwynne as 'MOTHER'S Her writing', was a Christmas pudding recipe, a hand-me-down that his mother headed 'Xmas Cake, Mrs Wheelers'. On Christmas Day, Gwynne served not one but two puddings – both sticky mounds soaked in brandy, Barbados sugar and Fowler's treacle, filled with almonds and dried fruits. One cake had been recently baked, the other made the previous year.[1]

Gwynne treasured the pleasures of family and home; as in life, these values formed the foundation of his architecture. The memories of his parents were happy ones: they had instilled in him curiosity and discipline. The proof was in the pudding, so to speak. How many parents would trust their 24-year-old to design and build them a country house? And one that in the late 1930s was in the cutting-edge modern style. 'When it was first built', recalled Gwynne in 1994 of The Homewood, 'it was extremely strange to a great many people'.[2] When gifting The Homewood to the National Trust, he stipulated that the house be lived in by a family.[3]

The Homewood was Gwynne's most notable architectural work: his home and office from its completion in 1938 until he died there in 2003. Over those many decades, he enriched the structure, interior and ten-acre woodland garden with fastidious care, leading his good friend, the architect Sir Denys Lasdun, to maintain that The Homewood was 'the great love of Patrick's life'.[4]

As Gwynne set ablaze his puddings on Christmas Day, the Welsh ancestral family whose fortune had financed The Homewood gazed down upon the festivities from the dining room wall. The older gentleman of the four Regency portraits, painted by the itinerant American Mather Brown and dating from about 1810, was the Revd Alban Thomas Gwynne, Lord of the Manor of Aberaeron and owner of the Monachty Estate, looking prosperous from building the new working harbour of Aberaeron on Cardigan Bay. He turns slightly towards his matronly second wife, Susannah Jones, who

In 1930, seeing the recently completed High and Over in Amersham, Buckinghamshire, by Amyas Connell, inspired the 17-year-old Gwynne to be an architect

is bedecked in a brightly beribboned cap, seemingly content as a wealthy heiress in her own right. They are accompanied by their dashing son Colonel Alban Gwynne, who had overseen the building of Aberaeron's pretty town squares and church, and his rosy-cheeked wife, Mary Anne, attired in a fashionable Empire dress of white muslin.

When Alban Patrick Gwynne was born on 25 March 1913 at the home his parents rented in Portchester, Hampshire, his father's fortune was not so secure.[5] Commander Alban Lewis Gwynne's income was split between modest rents from the Welsh estates and his career as a Royal Navy officer. Stationed at Portsmouth, he specialised in designing depth charges and naval mines while teaching at the Royal Navy's torpedo and mining school. More a technical landlubber than a sailor, he bemused visitors to The Homewood who often commented that the house looked like a giant ship by responding with the dry wit his son inherited that he hated the sea.

Neither Patrick nor his father used the name Alban. Lewis was known in the family as Dick (unknowing relations and friends calling him Richard), while Patrick's friends nicknamed him Algie, after his initials A L G.[6] Gwynne's beloved mother called her husband Gin, as the Turks mistakenly mispronounced his name when they first met on the dining terrace of a grand hotel in Constantinople. He had been seconded to help with naval mines as part of an unsuccessful effort to win the Ottoman Turks over to the British side before the First World War. Ruby Muriel Beatrice Bond was en route from India where she had been born, returning to Britain with her grandmother and recently widowed mother. In her early twenties, pretty with long hair piled high in tight curls, she was a third-generation colonial: her grandfather had gone to India as a cavalryman and her father had spent his whole life there, rising to the rank of colonel in the British Indian Army.[7] Ruby's life had been genteel and comfortable, surrounded by servants, summers spent in the cool climes of Simla, the vice-regal capital in the forested Himalayas where the upper crust of the British in India gathered.

Within a year of Patrick's birth, just before the outbreak of war in August 1914, the Gwynnes moved deep into the leafy Surrey countryside. Here the family rented and, several years later, purchased Homewood. A little less than two miles south of the pretty village of Esher and right on the Portsmouth Road, it afforded the Commander the choice of road or rail for his weekly commute to the naval base at Portsmouth. Gwynne remembered the Victorian house with mixed feelings. It had a big kitchen and many bedrooms with – unusual for the period – attached bathrooms, as well as day and night nurseries and servants' quarters. But with his developing modern tastes, he came to perceive an abuse of space and decoration; he judged the entrance hallway and staircase as 'useless' and said the plain cement exterior

Commander Alban Lewis and Mrs Ruby Gwynne, about 1910

with lines to imitate stone 'didn't fool anyone'. In Gwynne's eyes, Victorian architecture was always the enemy.[8]

Gwynne's sister Noreen Gwyneth was born soon after the move. As the new arrival, she was called Baby and, eventually, Babs. With only a year and half between them, and as the only children, Babs and Pat, as he was called by family and close friends, spent much time enjoying each other's company, cycling around the grounds, playing tennis on the court, swinging golf clubs and helping their father in the garden. The household was at first cared for with three live-in servants: a cook, housemaid and parlour maid. But few staff lasted long since Mrs Gwynne was, as her son proudly recollected, 'meticulous', with the need to do things well and to detail. This was a trait that he admitted picking up not only from her but also from his father; those friends and clients who came up against

Patrick's obsessive fastidiousness found in this gentle man a steely resolve that could be shifted only rarely.

Homewood was set in ten acres which Gwynne's father oversaw between his naval duties. Commander Gwynne worked directly alongside his full-time gardener and two hired boys in the upkeep of the ornamental garden around the house and, to support the estate, extensive market gardens. The mechanically minded Commander found great enjoyment in the combination of horticulture and garden machinery, filling notebooks with designs and planting tips, and advising others. In time, Gwynne took on these gifts and, alongside his architecture, added landscape in creating total design control in his schemes – from structure, to interior furnishings, to garden.

The setting of Homewood was delightful, in a dell cut by a meandering tributary of the nearby River Mole, the water usually narrow enough to jump over. The fringes of the property were all wooded. The entrance driveway curved off the Portsmouth Road around an ornamental pond surrounded by cypresses guarding the house. There were lawns and, protected by high walls and dotted with ornamental seating, a large formal garden with tall herbaceous borders. Beyond, to the west and south, was the tennis court, stands of old oaks and, notably, giant redwoods introduced from California, while rising on a gentle slope to the west, groves of birches. To the south, on several of the cleared acres, were an orchard and the market garden with storage buildings and the gardener's cottage.

While the Commander looked after the grounds, Mrs Gwynne tended to the household. Gwynne fondly remembered his mother's talent as a seamstress. She also rode well, with Babs taking after her, and even kept a horse at Homewood until it was stolen. Her singing voice was so good that her mother and grandmother had taken her when young to Milan for lessons. And she played the piano 'absolutely perfect[ly] … impeccably', Gwynne recalled, although he himself never got the hang of it when she tried to teach him. The appreciation of classical music, however, stayed with him, and a great number of his clients were musicians with a grand piano (or two), one even a world-famous pianist. Later in life, he replaced his mother's grand piano with an even better one for the pianist who came to live with him.

But one of Ruby's passions above all became Gwynne's – cuisine. Ruby had learnt to cook in India, a skill almost unheard of among women raised in households with servants, so that when the family were between cooks, Ruby could make an authentic Indian curry, one that become another of Gwynne's cherished recipes, with fresh ingredients straight from the family market garden. The young Patrick was raised on stories of his mother's visits to London, dining with the Commander at fashionable establishments like the

The old Victorian house at Homewood, Esher, when owned by the art collector Alexander Ionides, photographed by Bedford Lemere, 1890

Carlton Hotel with its rich French cuisine overseen by the famous Auguste Escoffier. There were also childhood visits to the large house in Queen's Gate of his wealthy Scottish godfather, James Baird, heir to the family's Russian ironworks in St Petersburg, where fine meals were prepared by the Italian head chef and his sous chef.

Ruby's cooking also helped during short periods of imposed economy, when, as Gwynne euphemistically styled it, his father was 'a bit pinched'. The Commander's income and financial ventures were not always enough to keep things afloat comfortably. Fees were required for Sandroyd, Patrick's preparatory school in nearby Cobham, and later for Harrow, so at times the big house had to be let. The family would then move into the old billiard room, a separate building near the house that had been converted into a cottage. Patrick did not enjoy having to watch others take over the family home, although he was intrigued by the more illustrious tenants and their guests. Princess Beatrice of Saxe-Coburg and Gotha, granddaughter of Queen Victoria and wife of the Spanish Infante Alfonso, took the house in the mid-1920s. The Infanta arrived with her three sons, princes Alvaro, Alfonso and Ataúlfo, so they too could attend Sandroyd. Gwynne would go up to the big house every Sunday evening to be driven with the princes back to school where they all boarded during the week. One Sunday, Princess Beatrice's sister was there, and Gwynne, to his embarrassment, found himself being kissed and called 'little darling' by Queen Marie of Romania. And although he did not see the dowager Queen Alexandra when she visited, Gwynne recalled that he did manage to spy Edward, Prince of Wales, the future King Edward VIII, with his latest girlfriend Freda Dudley Ward, through the hedge as he was 'larking around'. And, although he did not meet him, Albert Einstein lodged in Homewood during 1933 while he toured England for several weeks giving highly political talks, including at the Royal Albert Hall, just before making his permanent move to the United States.[9]

It was while at Harrow that Gwynne first became interested in architecture. He arrived aged 14, in 1927, and attended for three years. He was placed in Druries, a school boarding house where many other sons of naval officers lived; Old Druriens included the poet Lord Byron and Prime Minister Lord Palmerston. Gwynne was impressed when new formal steps and terraces appeared in front of the Old Schools building next door, the elegant design of the great imperial architect, Sir Herbert Baker; Gwynne likewise admired the Vaughan Library by Sir George Gilbert Scott, a neo-Gothic confection of Victorian architecture fairy-tale enough to seduce even this burgeoning modernist.

'I hope he will continue this improvement next term', wrote Gwynne's housemaster in his end of summer report for 1929. 'His drawing & painting are clearly good', although 'He still takes almost no part in any game'.[10] Gwynne avoided sports, and attending the Art Schools released him from football and cricket. He enjoyed sketching, drawing and painting in the school's fine purpose-built studio, adorned as it was on its outer walls with stone portrait medallions of William Hogarth and Sir Joshua Reynolds.

Gwynne liked to recall moments during his Harrow years which were formative to his becoming a modern architect. A visiting lecturer praised the new modernism and in his final year, 1929–30, his godfather gave him a subscription to the lavishly produced monthly *Architectural Review*, with its rare images of the latest flat-roofed, minimalist modern buildings from the Continent. British modernism – such as Charles Holden's London Underground designs – occasionally appeared amid more conservative local offerings. The 1930 Stockholm Exhibition, influential to many a budding

EARLY LIFE 1913-30

Patrick at Harrow School, age 14 in 1927

modernist of the period, received a full issue. Gwynne said it was the best introduction to modern architecture that he could have received: 'I wouldn't have met it anywhere else'.

Then came the architectural revelation, unsought. One leisurely day, motoring through the Chiltern Hills of Buckinghamshire with his mother, searching for things to sketch while also learning to drive, they arrived in Amersham and sighted a large white modern-looking building upon the summit of a hill. Approaching, they found a substantial country villa, extraordinarily planned in a Y shape, its façades starkly linear with elongated metal windows, crowned by flat-roof canopies cantilevered over its rooftop terrace. It was High and Over, one of the country's earliest modernist buildings, nearing completion in 1930. The architect was Amyas Connell (later to form the firm Connell Ward and Lucas), and this large country villa was his brilliant homage to the latest houses he had seen by leading modern architects in France. 'That sold me', Gwynne exclaimed.

Like most young people, Gwynne was excited by the latest trends. In 1930, modern was gaining an upper-case 'M', a seismic cultural shift that today we recognise as containing the ingredients of our contemporary world. Gwynne zestfully pursued the youthful lifestyle of dancing to early jazz records, tuning in to the latest music and world news on the wireless and enjoying the saucy wit of Noël Coward's plays. But above all, it was the hottest trends in architecture and design that captivated his curiosity.

In 1930, Gwynne left Harrow with prizes in design, watercolour and, showing his developing career ambitions, mechanical and architectural drawing. As prizes, he chose books on architecture. Yet Gwynne remembered his career choice more as a Damascene revelation. 'One day', he said, 'I just woke up and wanted to be an architect'. 'I never looked back from the moment I said, and it was quite sudden, that I wanted to be an architect. Nothing else was thought about.'

EARLY LIFE 1913–30

Commander Gwynne on his lawnmower in front of the old Homewood, about 1925

Patrick Gwynne's sister Noreen (Babs), about 1937

2   Becoming an architect, 1930–37

Directly upon leaving Harrow at 17 in the summer of 1930, Patrick Gwynne entered an architectural office. Instead of enrolling in a school of architecture, he chose pupillage, an unpaid apprenticeship (often the pupil having to pay) which was unusual by this date. His father sounded out friends who suggested Coleridge and Jennings, who had a reputable London office in Mayfair's North Audley Street when Gwynne joined, later moving to 21 Tothill Street near Westminster Abbey where the young novice found himself working in a bright sky-lit attic studio designed by the practice. The three architectural partners of the firm had emerged from the Arts and Crafts tradition and were accomplished if somewhat commercialised by the time Gwynne joined. Well connected through their upper-middle-class families, the brothers John Duke Coleridge (1879–1934) and Paul Humphrey Coleridge (1888–1955), descendants of the poet Samuel Taylor Coleridge, had teamed up with Frank Jennings (1877–1961), whose family's legal disputes had inspired Charles Dickens's *Bleak House*. John Duke Coleridge had been a pupil of Sir Edwin Lutyens, whose influence was visible in their houses and the smart suburban apartment blocks becoming popular by the time Gwynne joined. Jennings had a reputation for being a magpie architect, salvaging medieval timber and imaginatively incorporating it into large new houses.

These architects were not the most suitable choice for a promising modernist, and Gwynne later derided Manor Fields estate on Putney Hill, a big job in the office at the time – 228 flats in 14 blocks in the popular neo-Tudor style – as 'fake ... in a gentlemanly way'.[1] Claiming that he learned 'absolutely nothing' with the practice,[2] he took a cramming course to study structure and bought books on architecture and architectural history. But during his two years, he admitted to having learnt 'how to hold a pencil'. Jennings was the office's principal drawings man, working mostly in pencil while chain smoking, friendly to Gwynne and the other former public schoolboy pupil in the office. And, in all fairness, Gwynne would have picked up basics like filing, building procedures and sourcing of materials. At the end of the two years, he had earned the right to call himself an architect's

Gwynne, age 21, in his third car, a yellow and black Wolseley Hornet, motoring through Europe looking at modern architecture, 1933

Manor Fields, Putney, London, by Coleridge and Jennings, 1930–2. As an apprentice, Gwynne worked on this large estate of 14 mansion blocks

assistant. An older architect in the office, the émigré Mitrofan Soimenow from revolutionary Russia, encouraged his modern interests. When he and Gwynne were working together, Soimenow built a substantial house for himself in Petersham, near Richmond; long gone, Gwynne remembered it as in a style that 'might vaguely be called modern'.

At this period, Gwynne could almost count on his fingers the high modernists among London's architectural practitioners: there was, for example, Raymond McGrath, Joseph Emberton, Wells Coates, and the firm of Connell Ward and Lucas. Erich Mendelsohn came from Germany in 1933 and formed a partnership with Serge Chermayeff, followed in 1934 by the founder of the Bauhaus, Walter Gropius, who practiced with Maxwell Fry, and then Marcel Breuer arrived and joined F R S Yorke a year later. After placing an advertisement in an architectural journal saying he wanted to be in a modern practice, Gwynne got a single response, from Mendelsohn, who invited him to his office in the Pantheon Building on Oxford Street.

The meeting did not go well. Mendelsohn made a rather cutting remark about a set of design drawings for a house with steel windows that Gwynne brought to show him. And the great man said he had no openings. Turning the experience on its head, Gwynne would later say that it was Mendelsohn who 'didn't appeal'. He thought Mendelsohn just wanted to see the man who placed such an advert.

Meanwhile, Commander Gwynne, trying yet another financial venture, had been appointed a director of Stic B, a new French company specialising in paint for stonework, then mainly used on modern buildings (and still in production today).[3] In the absence of architectural work, Patrick became an employee, travelling about in a van and scaling ladders for an enjoyable two and a half years painting buildings. Always itching to design, he convinced the Stic B managers to let him use an attic space in the office outside working hours as a studio and, with permission, had letterheaded paper printed with the company's prestigious Westminster office address of 14 Palmer Street, calling himself an architect.[4] With a wide and affluent set of friends and acquaintances, and with plenty of building plots available, there was always someone toying with the idea for a new house. Although nothing came of any of these early projects, Gwynne had begun his experiments in domestic design.

If he could not yet build big, he could build small, for himself and the family. In 1934, Gwynne fitted out several spaces in Homewood, his first executed interiors. Contemporary photographs only hint that the modern fitments and furnishings are in a Victorian house. Under the sloping ceiling of his attic bedroom he installed a new magazine rack and flat-fronted cabinet with long chrome pull-handles. In the spacious entrance hall, he made every effort to remove dated features and to streamline raised surfaces by setting doors flush to the wall. He experimented with new materials like aluminium in his designs for wall-mounted uplighters and chromium for fascias. A few pieces of bent plywood furniture by Alvar Aalto added the new look that Gwynne found in the pages of the *Architectural Review*.

Working in his time off from painting, Gwynne prepared the winning design for a furniture competition in 1935 sponsored by B Cohen and Sons, a large and well-established furniture maker in Shoreditch. The competition judges were big names in the design field: Max Fry, the respected design historian John Gloag, as well as H de C Hastings, editor of the *Architectural Review* and *Architects' Journal* who published the winning design. As a promotion, Cohen decided to manufacture Gwynne's proposals for a table lamp and a curving aluminium furniture frame reminiscent of Aalto's forms; his father's technical expertise in metals helped with the detailing.[5] But Gwynne quickly discovered that the whole exercise was a publicity stunt and only a few lamps were made.

PATRICK GWYNNE

Top left: Gwynne's alterations to the hall at the old Homewood, 1934

Above and left: Gwynne modernised his bedroom under the eaves of the old Homewood, 1934

First-prize entry, Cohen furniture competition, 1935

On occasion, Gwynne put aside his painter's apron and donned evening dress. He knew many 'well-to-do daughters' who were 'coming out' on the debutante dance circuit before being presented at Court. Some were sisters of his young male friends or girlfriends of his sister Babs, who was also on the circuit. The balls were fun, 'very grandly done' in large town and country houses. On weekends, friends would often stay at Homewood. One friendship that Gwynne kept up from Harrow was with John Profumo, although they rarely saw each other after the infamous scandal of the 'Profumo Affair' of 1963 helped bring down the Conservative government.

And motoring became a lifelong passion. His mother had been an early woman driver and taught her husband as well as Patrick to drive. At 17, his parents gave him a convertible Austin 7 Taylor Semi-Sports, in flashy red and silver, his first in a long line of sports cars, including several Aston Martins, all of which he drove notoriously fast but skilfully. For his 21st birthday in 1933, Gwynne's parents presented him with a yellow and black Wolseley Hornet, his third open-top car. With his Harrovian friend Brian Coates, he took off to tour the Continent. Landing in Belgium, they followed a route east through France, Germany, Switzerland and on to Vienna. Photographs of the pair bathing together on the shores of Lake Lucerne, wearing little or nothing, recall the images of young gay men in a free Europe on the edge of cataclysm, so well portrayed in Christopher Isherwood's *Goodbye to Berlin* (1939) and its musical adaptation *Cabaret*. Looking at architecture, old and very new, they sought out the sleek modernism of the Schocken department store (1926) in Stuttgart by Mendelsohn, where they found themselves surrounded by a nasty gang of young Nazis who goaded them for photographing 'a Jewish store'.[6] Very influential on Gwynne's fledging modernist tastes was a visit to the Weissenhof Estate on the hilly outskirts of the city, a Mount Olympus of modern white houses by the new architectural gods including Le Corbusier, Mies van der Rohe, Gropius, Bruno Taut and Hans Poelzig. The geometric forms and pared-down constructional aesthetic of the buildings perfectly voiced the architectural language that Gwynne was seeking.

Back among the small group of painters at Stic B, Gwynne befriended a Russian refugee who had a friend connected to some of the modern architects practicing in London. In 1935, Gwynne found himself at a party in Notting Hill, surreptitiously held for his job-seeking benefit by the Swedish Count Eric Lewenhaupt and his painter wife Dora.[7] Gwynne fell into conversation with Marion Coates, who introduced him to her husband, the architect Wells Coates. Gwynne thought him charming and easy-going, so he asked for a job and was invited to visit the office a week later. It was his big break.

At the interview, Coates looked over Gwynne's portfolio and offered him a three-week trial period, at £2 10s a week. This was half of what the other draughtsmen were earning, but Gwynne was pleased by the prospect of working for one of Britain's major modernists. He was immediately assigned to draw up small details for the entrances of the 11-storey Embassy Court on Brighton's seafront and Lawn Road Flats in Hampstead. The London block is Coates's best-known work: a sleek concrete mass with metal windows, distinguished by bold external walkways and stairs. Gropius and his wife lived in the building during their short London period and other notable émigrés passed through. On its opening in 1937, the Isobar on the ground floor became London's hotspot for many experimental architects and designers. Gwynne's humble contribution was to detail the desk in the entrance hall.

Wells Coates (1895–1958) was an attractive if complex character. He had entered architecture through mechanical engineering and held a doctorate on the subject of diesel engines. His machine-driven outlook complemented the new architecture and appealed to Gwynne who, like his father, relished technical solutions. In fact, Commander Gwynne and Coates came to enjoy each other's company, sharing an interest in ships, the Commander even helping Coates on one of his boat designs. Coates's parents were Canadian Methodist missionaries who lived pious and relatively austere lives; his father was a professor of theology, his mother a nutritionist. He was born and spent his early years in Tokyo, raised speaking Japanese, and encouraged to cultivate an appreciation for Japanese culture that embraced *shibui*, an aesthetic of beauty found through simplicity, balance and contrast, traditional qualities that came to shape Coates's approach to architecture and design.

Coates played a key role in the network of major modern architects at home and abroad. In Paris, he courted Le Corbusier. In 1931, he briefly visited the Bauhaus in Dessau and in 1933, two years before Gwynne joined his office, he had been instrumental in forming the Modern Architectural Research Group (MARS), a pressure group of critics and architects allied to the Congrès Internationaux d'Architecture Moderne founded in 1928.

Coates's office was at 15 Coastal Chambers, Elizabeth Street, part of the development of the new Victoria Coach Station by Wallis, Gilbert and Partners. It was a building today considered Art Deco, a style that those in the office, said Gwynne, 'loathed … it was not Modern Movement … it was modern in as much as it wasn't classical fake of any sort'. As for Wallis Gilbert's famous Firestone building, Gwynne dismissed it as a 'comic façade in front of a factory … no more to us than someone doing Bogus Tudor'. But Coastal Chambers had big windows, and against these, perched in a row at their drawing boards, were Gwynne and a half dozen other young architects. The drawing office was long and narrow, divided at points by elegant glass screens, behind one of which sat Coates and his secretary. Along the back wall, 'very nicely done', Gwynne said, and 'new to us in that day', were displayed building materials, 'not useful at all but the sort of nice display people put on'. Positioned on shelves and window ledges around the office were radios designed by Coates for E K Cole Limited, including his classic circular Bakelite EKCO AD-65. Coates was very much involved in furniture and product design, creating tubular-steel furniture for the popular Practical Equipment Limited, known as PEL, and radiograms for EMG Handmade Gramophones Limited. When Gwynne was launching his solo career, he would draw upon Coates's connections for jobs with some of these companies.

Joining soon after Gwynne was Denys Lasdun (1914–2001), fresh from his studies at the Architectural Association. The two became lifelong friends. The architectural career of Lasdun, later Sir Denys, would skyrocket after 1960 with his Royal College of Physicians and National Theatre. Among the other talented young architects in the office were Acheson Best Overend (1907–77), John Wheeler (1915–45), Edric Neel (1914–52) and Rodney Thomas (1906–96); during the war Neel and Thomas formed the respected Arcon group, designing prefabricated houses and working in early plastics. The atmosphere around the office was 'jolly nice', said Gwynne.

Everyone was charmed by Coates. He was man of excellent taste, well travelled and, being skilled in shorthand and typing, was able to produce articles quickly for journals and books. Although Lasdun characterised him as 'vain' and much attracted to the ladies, he held him in high esteem as an architect, impressed by how Coates would think and design in section. And Lasdun also appreciated, as did Gwynne, Coates's striking attention to detail as he 'blurred design and technology.'[8]

After an initial three-week probation, Coates called Gwynne in and told him how pleased he was with his progress and increased his salary to £3. This made Gwynne chuckle because, as he said, 'it was a rotten salary'. But for all his activity, Coates had little ready cash: poor financial management dogged his career and eventually drove him to live in Canada.

Wells was as mad about cars as Gwynne and both drove Wolseley Hornets, Gwynne suffering mild embarrassment as his was a marginally superior model. Wells upgraded to an open two-seater Lancia that Gwynne thought so suited him that 'he could have designed it himself'. But then Gwynne unintentionally one-upped Coates and bought his dream car, a new 1937 open-top Talbot 3.5 Litre Tourer Roadster at a bargain £550 (the price of a respectable London terrace house at the time); it was, admitted Gwynne, an 'over-designed car but it was an absolute beauty'.[9]

The year 1937 was a very busy and momentous one for Gwynne. First, he was put in charge of supervising the fabrication of a studio living space for Coates, who had recently separated from his wife. The top floor of the two-storey Victorian terrace house at 18 Yeoman's Row, near Harrods, was gutted and totally redesigned. In the history of British modern architecture, this little flat became celebrated both for its ingenious design and the parties that Coates threw. Gwynne drew most of the working drawings, helped source materials, and supervised building works. The flat was open-plan and lit by large double-height windows. Most of the space was given over to living and dining areas and, prominently placed, a mobile typing desk that could be stored away in a wall unit, an idea later lifted by Gwynne for his own secretary. The mezzanine bedroom was accessed by a metal ladder. Almost all the fixtures and furnishings were built-in. Coates lived in the studio until 1958; Gwynne was invited to gatherings, the host showing off his flair for cooking and entertainment, much as Gwynne increasingly did.[10]

In 1937 too, Gwynne assisted in the drawings for 10 Palace Gate, a block of flats near Kensington Gardens. Although Gwynne never mentioned the flats when reminiscing, a drawing survives which he initialled as his work and Neel signed for the revision.[11] Coates, checking a print of the drawing, picked up a coloured pencil and sketched out the dimensions on the elevations and sections showing the 3:2 ratio that caught the attention of the

BECOMING AN ARCHITECT, 1930–37

Wells Coates in his Yeoman's Row studio flat in 1937, photographed by Howard Coster. Gwynne supervised the construction of the flat when working in Coates's office.

In 1937, Gwynne oversaw the drawings and construction of Wells Coates's design for Shipwrights, Benfleet, Essex

profession as an innovation in flat design. Gwynne would soon manipulate Coates's use of proportional planning in designing The Homewood.

Next came Gwynne's largest project in the office, overseeing the drawings and construction of a house for John Wyborn, the director of EKCO for whom Coates designed his famous radios. Three or four times a week, Gwynne was on site at Shipwrights in Benfleet, Essex, fashioning this white box raised on Corbusian pilotis. The interior displayed Coates's expertise in fitted cabinets and wall-to-wall shelving. Like all the projects he worked on in Coates's office, Shipwrights gave Gwynne access to builders and craftsmen who understood and could execute modern forms – most cabinetmakers of the period were trained in free-standing pieces, stained and lacquered, not in curved, precision-cut timber units favoured by the modernists.

As 1937 wore on, Wells Coates's financial problems worsened; he reduced staff in the autumn and closed the office in February 1938.[12] To merge resources, Coates, Gwynne, Lasdun and Neel became associates. Gwynne later recalled: 'we were all supposed to pool our work, and I did to some

BECOMING AN ARCHITECT, 1930–37

Mews house for art dealer
Peter Klaus von Krauschen near
Marble Arch, London, 1937

PATRICK GWYNNE

Drawing room for Dr Langdale Clarke, Bruton Street, Mayfair, London, 1937

extent on The Homewood ... [Coates] pooled his name with mine ... But he really got no work and he had to close his office, and so there wasn't an associateship, we had do to something [each] ourselves'. The three young architects and Coates took an office in Sloane Street, and Gwynne put up their names on a plate outside, although Coates often worked from his studio and Gwynne at Homewood to save coming into town.

During this associateship Gwynne undertook several interiors for 'bachelor friends'. He labelled the jobs 'very straightforward showroom stuff', indicating that they were apartments of fashionable display. One client was Peter Klaus von Krauschen, an art dealer and recent émigré from Germany who still craved his home country's modernism. Gwynne stripped the Victorian features from von Krauschen's small London mews house near Marble Arch and gave it a sleek interior of long, fitted wall cabinets with surfaces illuminated by concealed lights. One side of the house overlooked a pretty church cemetery, but the other had a poor aspect onto the street, so Gwynne masked the window with a translucent internal screen that could be lit at night.

In Bruton Street, Mayfair, Gwynne modernised a first-floor drawing room for a Scottish doctor, Langdale Clarke, with its grand piano, fur-covered Bruno Mathsson bentwood chaises longues, and a fine radio cabinet by Gwynne that rivalled similar designs by Coates. Off one wall hung a cocktail cabinet, internally lit and mirror backed, with a central drop flap and flanking wooden tambour doors which were to become a feature of many of Gwynne's fittings. Similarly, several of the walls were covered in Japanese grass paper, a surface treatment that became almost a trademark of Gwynne's interiors.[13]

And then, finally, during the autumn of 1937, Patrick Gwynne embarked upon what would be his masterwork, The Homewood. He was 24 years old.

3 The Homewood 1937–39

Over a two-year period from 1936, Commander Gwynne sold his Welsh ancestral properties in Aberaeron. They had brought in a rent of £1,200 a year, and with the sale and wise investment by a stockbroker cousin, the Gwynnes finally achieved financial stability. They could now afford to build a new house, trusting in their son.

They had always found the Victorian villa too close to the busy road, so much so that 'the crockery bounced on the table', and therefore sought to move, looking as far as Kent. But failing to find something suitable, and with the Commander feeling too old to plant out another garden, the family decided to build anew elsewhere on their land and then demolish the old house. They chose a point at the intersection of the L-shaped property, looking down both arms, far from the road and on a slight rise where the rhododendron maze stood. This position faced south over a treed lawn which screened the market garden beyond.

Gwynne joked that he sold his architectural ideas to his parents 'from breakfast to dinner'. They were indulgent, accepting completely the idea that the house would be in his modern taste. He took on board his mother's request for a kitchen divided into three areas because the staff sometimes got territorial in one space, and also that the principal rooms be traditionally planned, for example a dining room separated from the living space. But there it ended: 'I imposed quite a bit on them, such as the size of rooms'.

In September 1937, Gwynne was still in loose partnership with Wells Coates, Denys Lasdun and Edric Neel, although each was doing their own projects. For the new house, Coates suggested that Gwynne draw up a design based upon his Sunspan houses, a speculative house type that Coates had first exhibited in 1934 at the *Daily Mail* Ideal Home Exhibition. The houses had proved popular, but were not on the grand scale and in the high modern style that Gwynne was seeking. Patrick roughed one up, but his father rejected the sketch in favour of the design that was eventually built. Coates made a few small suggestions but, said Gwynne, 'he wasn't in on it at all'.[1] Naturally, Gwynne tapped into Coates for useful contacts in the

Looking down the terrazzo stairwell to the sunken uplighter, The Homewood

building trade, and there is no doubt that the influence of Coates's style and detailing can be seen throughout the house, but it was only when The Homewood was finished – 'The' now added to the house name – and they were walking around the garden, did Coates ask that his name appear alongside that of Gwynne in an upcoming publication, and placed first. A little ruffled, as he recounted, Gwynne turned to his father, who told him not to quarrel. The outcome is that many scholars place The Homewood in Coates's *oeuvre*.[2]

Gwynne made the architectural drawings for the house from a small hut in the garden, feeding the sheets to the workmen as construction progressed. At tender stage he drew at 1/16" scale, but for the working drawings he moved on to the more detailed 1/8", and even 1/4". He oversaw the work of the contractors and subcontractors, vigilantly ensuring details were carried out accurately in execution. The Homewood was completed in nine months, an incredibly rapid schedule for such a substantial house; even Gwynne himself would later recollect his youthful energy in quiet disbelief.

The family – Commander and Mrs Gwynne, Patrick and Babs, and Ruby's mother, Mrs Wilhelmina Bond, known to the family as Aunt Mina, who had come to live with them – all celebrated with a housewarming party in July 1938, dinner being served on the terrace as the house was not yet fully ready for occupancy. The Homewood had cost £10,500, approximately 20 times the price of the average UK house at that time.[3]

The Homewood made its published debut in a comprehensive 14-page spread in the September 1939 issue of the *Architectural Review*, with Gwynne's name placed before Coates in the credit.[4] With excellent photographs by Dell and Wainwright, the premier architectural photographers of the day, and extensive plans, detail drawings and photomontages created by Gwynne, as well as an explanatory text heavily reliant upon the architect's notes, The Homewood's unveiling was stylishly controlled by its architect.

Gwynne had thoroughly photographed the construction of the superstructure with its steel-rod reinforced concrete laid in slabs and piers and set upon 10-foot piles – unusually deep, Gwynne said, to prevent it from 'sliding down the hill'.[5] Exterior surfaces were painted, plastered or clad in brick. Needless to say, the rendered surfaces were painted in Stic B. The consulting structural engineer was Felix Samuely, a brilliant innovator who collaborated with many prominent modern architects of the period – he had, for example, worked on Coates's Palace Gate flats, and Mendelsohn and Chermayeff's Bexhill De La Warr Pavilion. Cyril Sweett was the quantity surveyor, again an important figure among the progressive moderns, a key player in the MARS Group.

Construction sequence of The Homewood photographed by Gwynne, 1938

1938

APR

APR

MAY

PATRICK GWYNNE

Staircase block, reflected in the pool designed by Denys Lasdun, The Homewood, 1938

Gwynne created a plan with a highly articulated division of the three main functions of domestic life: living, sleeping and services (see p.141). All the principal rooms are on the upper of the two storeys to take advantage of the views. Two wings lie at right-angles to one another, linked by the block enclosing a beautiful terrazzo spiral staircase, a space lit in the day from the glazed wall to the garden terrace, and at night by a sunken circular light. The east wing tapers away from the entrance block so as not to overwhelm it, and accommodates suites of bedrooms on the upper floor and, at ground level, the entrance hall, a small WC, a flower-arranging room and Commander Gwynne's study. The larger L-shaped main block is dominated by the expansive living room, with its wall of glass affording views south over the garden, and at the west end, the dining room, able to be closed off by a curtain, later replaced by a folding screen wall. On the north are the kitchen and staff quarters with a four-car garage below.

The exterior – flat roofed, white, lying long and low on the garden rise – articulates the two wings and conjoining staircase block. The protruding bedroom and study wing is Gwynne's homage to Shipwrights, similar in appearance to Coates's house on the inner side to the patio, with its thin line of upper-storey windows over the pilotis and intervening voids. The east façade finds inspiration in Le Corbusier's villas of the 1920s, above all the

THE HOMEWOOD 1937–39

Porte cochère and bedroom wing, The Homewood, 1938

The kitchen

The garden front of The Homewood upon completion in 1938

Villa Savoye, which Gwynne acknowledged 'was something I was looking at all the time', particularly for the bedroom wing, 'although it's based on the style not the plan, of course, because the plan to be honest is a silly plan although I adore the house, a piece of sculpture really'. Gwynne's twist was to punctuate the long horizontal strip of windows with a pair of balconies which he described as 'pulled-out pieces of concrete-like drawers'.

The interior was restrained luxury.[6] The great living room at the heart of the house was created for family and entertainment. During the day, light floods the room through the south window, a wall of glass set in teak frames. The opposite wall is a custom built-in unit, originally in French walnut, of illuminated display shelves, and compartments with tambour doors concealing a built-in radiogram and record collection. It also has a food hatch opening through to the kitchen, with an ingeniously concealed serving table beneath, which drops out when needed. The west wall is of dark green figured marble inset with the fireplace recess, the design derived from Gwynne's seeing photographs of Mies van der Rohe's buildings like the Barcelona Pavilion of 1929 and especially, as the architect acknowledged, the

'Living & Dining Room', from presentation boards of collaged drawings and photographs made by Gwynne for publication, 1938

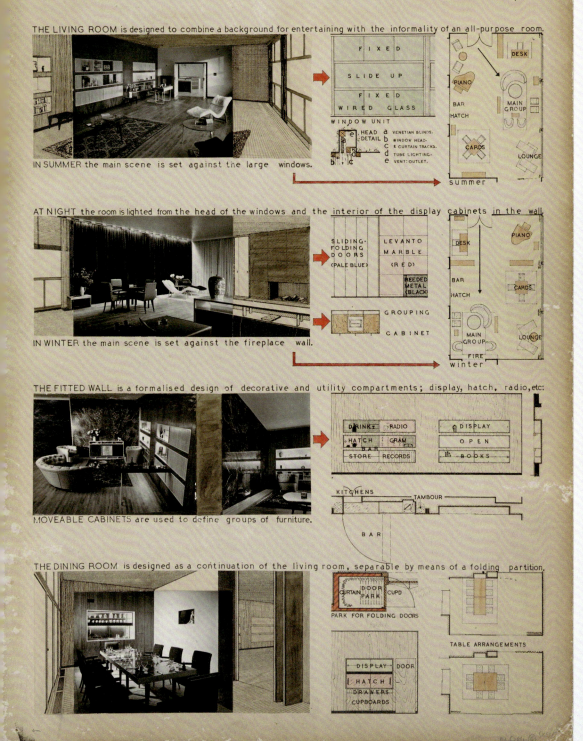

PATRICK GWYNNE

Living room with seating in front of the marble fireplace wall

The floor-to-ceiling windows of the living room with a pair of Bruno Mathsson chaises longues

'very influential' Tugendhat House of 1928–30 that he knew from his copy of F R S Yorke's *The Modern House* (1934). The wall of windows is also somewhat inspired by the Tugendhat House but even more by Coates's 10 Palace Gate, with Coates helping Gwynne secure the windows from the same Austrian supplier. The living room came to life when Mrs Gwynne sat down to play the grand piano in the corner of the room, or the furniture was pushed aside for dancing on the sprung maple floor.

In the adjoining dining room, walls were veneered in walnut, and there is a counter with a hotplate and a hatch through to the servery. The west wall was fully glazed, with a sliding door giving access to the balcony and a metal staircase with teak treads leading down to the garden. From the balcony too, a small spiral staircase led on to the roof where Gwynne had arranged a roof deck for sunbathing in front of a curved canvas screen hiding the water tanks – sun worshipping, Gwynne recalled, was then 'new, and you felt you had to hide'.

The extensive bedroom wing contained an arrangement of small rooms finely fitted out. A third of the upper level was given over to Commander and Mrs Gwynne's suite of a sleeping room, boudoir, dressing room, bathroom and WC. There were bedrooms for Patrick and Babs, and two for guests, as well as further bathrooms, cloakrooms and WCs, some with borrowed light from the glass-brick partitions on the corridor. The sixth bedroom was a last-minute addition made for Mrs Gwynne's mother, designed while building was underway, an indication of Gwynne's adaptability during construction. Because Babs complained that there was never enough room in the old house for her and her friends to do their hair and makeup, especially if there was a party, Gwynne provided a powder room neatly tucked behind the circular wall of the staircase, looking like a theatrical dressing room, with a long counter sprouting a pair of circular mirrors on fixed stands.

Gwynne designed the furniture, from beds to leather-top desks. Built-in fitments, such as wardrobes and bedside table units, were finished in French walnut, birch and mahogany. The detailing throughout was exceptional, down to the illuminated compartment with its tambour-door hatchway for the telephone in the main suite. Much of the work was carried out by a firm of London cabinetmakers, as was the free-standing furniture that Gwynne designed throughout the house, including the dining room table as well as the desk, card table and coffee table in the living room, and all were built under the direction of Leslie Bilsby (1911–90) with his connections in the building trades.

In Gwynne's career, Bilsby came to play an important role as builder, developer and friend, introducing Gwynne to many clients and using him as his own architect for three houses. They had met through Coates, who had taken his office team to an exhibition of modern furniture assembled

PATRICK GWYNNE

The master dressing room with built-in vanity and wardrobe

by Chermayeff at Whiteley's Department Store in Bayswater – it was 'stunning' in Gwynne's recollection. Bilsby ran building and design sales for the store, and he and Coates got to know one another. Coates hired Bilsby to manage some of his building jobs, a few of which Gwynne worked on, including the Yeoman's Row studio. Bilsby soon developed friendships with the young staff, who were his contemporaries, thus coming to serve as a project manager for the 'associates' when Coates closed his office.[7] In 1938, when working on The Homewood, Bilsby was doing similar project management with Lasdun on the architect's first major house at 32 Newton Road, while also assisting Neel on a large exhibition stand in Glasgow. He also worked for Ernö Goldfinger, building and fitting out 1–3 Willow Road in Hampstead.

From Coates, Gwynne had grasped the concept of grids and modules, assigning a given proportion when designing The Homewood in a system of his own devising. The use of ratio in architectural design is as old as architecture itself, providing balance and harmony, but the moderns, most famously Le Corbusier, promoted their own versions relating to constructional and functional requirements. Regulated pattern, Gwynne recognised, mirrored the discipline he required to express space. It is 'the sort of thing I love', he said; 'I really rather need a discipline'. From 1937, proportion and ratio would form the basis of Gwynne's architecture, sometimes quite simple, at other times, complex and perplexing. 'There are very few things I haven't done without some sort of guiding thing of that sort', he remarked. 'We were always getting out our set-square ... if I get a grid going it tells all the time even if you don't notice.'[8]

The article in the *Architectural Review* devoted a whole page to detailed drawings and photographs illustrating the basis of Gwynne's grid design. His golden mean was a vertical module of 1 foot 8 inches and a horizontal of 4-foot units, and these he multiplied and arranged together in harmonic configurations. The first-floor garden front is divided into five sections, each composed of 3 × 4-foot modules. Exterior and interior plans, elevations and sections conform to these units. To use a 4-foot module was, Gwynne admitted, 'quite extravagant'.

His use of colour for The Homewood was more relaxed. Colour was always important for Gwynne, and in these early years he experimented with colour theory. Le Corbusier was a leading inspiration, especially when he collaborated with the French artist Amédée Ozenfant in defining a style they termed Purism, a variation on Cubism that spoke of abstracting objects into geometric shapes and highlighting them through colour. This is what Gwynne did at The Homewood. He knew of Ozenfant and his theories, as did many British architects, the painter having moved recently to London and published six articles in the *Architectural Review* in 1937.

ALG
HOUSE AT ESHER
ARCHITECTS PATRICK GWYNNE & WELLS COATES

FACADE DESIGN
showing controlling "grid".

EAST

A EQUALS 1'8", 2A 3'4" CILL, 3A 5'0", 4A 6'8" HEAD, 5A 8'4" CEILING, 6A 10'0" CEILING ...ETC:
B EQUALS 4'0".

SOUTH

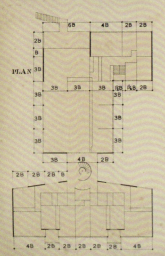
PLAN

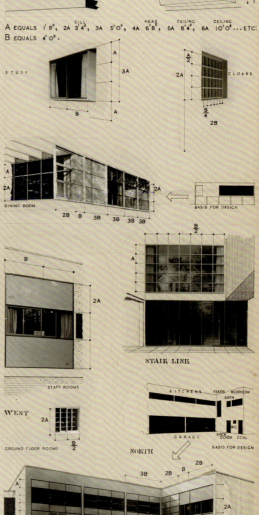

Gwynne was partial to the use of solid colour and rarely used decorative patterns for textiles and wallpapers, although he was not averse to wide contrasting stripes in his early years. In the *Architectural Review*, he carefully articulated The Homewood's colours, describing 'concrete painted ivory white', the soffit 'pale blue', the balcony windows 'brick red', 'grey steel frames', the dining-room end wall 'rendered in a warm buff colour with inset chocolate lines divided into panels'. Colours invariably came with a descriptive adjective or hue: yellow is 'mustard yellow', black is 'ebonised'. While more intuitive than systematic in his approach, Gwynne owned a box of mix-and-match paint chip cards titled *The Unesma Colour Plates (Approved by late Mr Ostwald)*, made in Germany about 1934 and distributed by the English art products company Winsor and Newton. Friedrich Wilhelm Ostwald (1856–1932) was a Latvian-born chemist and Nobel prize winner, an influential colour theorist who had lectured at the Bauhaus. Gwynne's set contained 36 related colour hues arranged in triangular formation on 26 sheets. Gwynne even made little cards of his own for isolating the colours, and although any literal adoption of the system to his work is tenuous, the plates do show him thinking and experimenting with colour relationships. Controlled and understood, colour always played an important role in his architecture, interiors and garden designs.

The context of The Homewood in the landscape was also an important design consideration, especially since the property was extensive and established. Commander Gwynne worked with his son to open up a new driveway to the house, bordering it with specialist rhododendrons to create a spectacular spring show. In contemporary articles and books, Gwynne studied the novel geometric garden designs appearing in Britain and on the Continent.[9] The paved terraces around the house had symmetrical planting squares which each year he filled with a meticulously chosen colour arrangement of begonias (as they still are). The highlight of the south terrace was an oval ornamental pool designed by Lasdun, placed on axis with the staircase block, a housewarming gift to Patrick's parents.

Early in 1940, Professor Charles Reilly reviewed the new houses of the past year and included The Homewood, which he knew only from photographs. Not an easy critic, he called it 'thrilling' and 'part of a new world', although he seemed amused by its modern transparency: 'I cannot help feeling one must be under forty with a good figure and no bad habits to enjoy oneself thoroughly in this plate-glass world'.[10]

'Façade Design', from presentation boards of collaged drawings and photographs made by Gwynne for publication, 1938

4 The war and mid-century modern, 1940–59

The Gwynne family had enjoyed only one year in The Homewood when in September 1939 the Second World War broke out. As a First World War veteran, the Commander was automatically recalled to active duty and at first was given small jobs like censoring mail at the Admiralty in Whitehall; then, as things became established, he returned to design as a submarine mine engineer posted to the Isle of Skye, an uncomfortable remote location to be at the age of 60. Babs joined the Women's Royal Naval Service and was stationed mainly in London, but later was assigned to the South East Asian Command under Lord Mountbatten in Ceylon, moving with him as one of his personal assistants to (with shades of her mother's ancestry) India. Patrick, in June 1940, joined the Royal Air Force Volunteer Reserve (RAFVR), entering at the initial rank of pilot officer.

Mrs Gwynne was thus left at home with her ailing mother who lived until April 1943. Worried that The Homewood might be requisitioned by the army, with visions, Gwynne said, of 'hobnail boots' tearing up the hardwood floors, the family rented the house furnished, with Mrs Gwynne moving once again to the former billiard room cottage. Writing to Patrick, she said that the first tenants appeared suitable – they had two Rolls Royces. But they turned out to be destructive, using the good crockery for shooting practice over the lawn. They were, Patrick intoned, 'self-made potted meat manufacturers who had gone very grand'. They stayed a year until replaced by the architect Robert Lutyens, son of Sir Edwin Lutyens, the most celebrated establishment architect of the time. On the day of the viewing, Babs showed the prospective tenant, his wife and the 71-year-old Sir Edwin around the house, 'which was quite amusing', Patrick recalled, as she 'wondered what the old boy would say' since The Homewood was so very much divorced from both Sir Edwin's famous Arts and Crafts houses and his neoclassical buildings. Lutyens' famous wit failed with Babs when, looking at the great living room windows, he quipped, 'the architect doesn't seem to know that

Gwynne's gouache design drawing for a house competition held by the Canadian Wood Association, 1957

you don't put glass down to the floor'. Realising his faux pas, he apologised saying that the house was 'not quite his sort of architecture, but very good of its sort'. However, Mrs Gwynne found the Lutyenses to be excellent tenants, fond of the house and staying a year. The next tenants were Norwegians who understandably 'loved it', said Patrick, as he credited all Scandinavians as having good modern taste. The last tenant was the Chilean ambassador Manuel Bianchi, who remained until Patrick and Babs returned from the war.

The untimely deaths of both Commander and Mrs Gwynne in 1942, within ten days of each other, was a tragedy. Patrick's mother had been ill for some while, but his father's death from prostate cancer was unexpected. As Patrick said, 'they barely lived in the house'.[1] At the time of their deaths, he was overseas, serving with his RAF training aircrew on his first major posting at a small flying station outside Assiniboia, Saskatchewan, Canada, and so his sister Babs had to deal with all the heart-breaking arrangements.

The two words that Gwynne used repeatedly when describing his wartime experiences were 'pleasant' and 'boring', an emotional combination often found in camp life where the stimulation of daily activities is tempered by waiting for something to happen. His duties were administrative, and in Canada centred around the training of pilots. Assiniboia ('pleasant') was very isolated, in the midst of the vast and sparsely populated Canadian prairies; it was a 'shock for the eye', Gwynne recalled, with bitterly cold winters and hot summers. Entertainment had to be self-made, usually plays and music, Gwynne volunteering to create a proscenium arch for the drill hall stage, which was well made by the expert carpenters skilled in working on the aeroplanes. It had modern columns, Gwynne recalled. After just over a year in Western Canada he was made Chief Administration Officer, second in authority to the Commanding Officer, and posted to the flying training unit at Goodrich, Ontario in Eastern Canada ('pleasant'). Here again he found a small bit of design work, replacing the tiny food serving hatch in the officers' mess with a long length of stainless steel counter for cooking and serving, an open arrangement that Gwynne considered 'was frightfully modern for those days', foreshadowing his specialisation in designing catering spaces.

Goodrich was only a short flight or train journey to Toronto from which Gwynne and his squadron friends were able to catch a train to New York City, where, as allied forces, they found themselves given free tickets for the best seats in the theatre. Gwynne also journeyed down the east coast by train as far as Miami, where he had one of his friends use his camera to photograph him on a palm-tree beach wearing snazzy-patterned swimming trunks. The photo was in colour, taken on 35mm Kodachrome slide film, a new product then only available to American amateur photographers. Expensive cameras were another of Gwynne's interests, to be succeeded by home movie cameras.

RAF Squadron Leader Gwynne on a Florida beach, about 1943

Gwynne appreciated that he was serving away from the fighting and far from war-torn Britain, although naturally there was 'a slight feeling of guilt'. In a typewritten letter to his Aunt Gladys, one of his father's two sisters, he marvelled at her talent at growing tomatoes in her drawing room, while sharing his thoughts about building for the future, mixing the pessimism and optimism of those dark days. Gloomily he asks, 'Will we assume no future wars? Can one do that except in idealistic moments? I like to think so but is it wise? One cannot go H. G. Wells and live below the ground.' Then, with hope: 'I would pay no attention to the possibility of future wars in my town planning, county planning or roadmaking ... In fact, the more one surveys the future the more it appears that a well-planned city will because of its planning be a safe city' if those 'with vested interests' (citing the Duke of Westminster, the major landlord of London's wealthy Mayfair district) 'will allow it', which Gwynne seemed to doubt.[2]

In early 1944, Gwynne returned to England, lodging at a camp near Manchester ('boring'), before transferring to another near Dumfries, Scotland ('pleasant'), and finally in October, to a tented camp in Kent ('frozen camp bed'). From there he took part in the Allied push through north-west Europe, landing in Belgium ('very boring'), on to 'a funny little place in France which really might not have been France, no sort of food in those days', before entering occupied Germany ('extremely dreary, defeated Germans'). VE Day found him in Eindhoven in the Netherlands admiring 'the meticulous brickwork, in drives, paths, streets, and the good condition of planting'.[3]

Squadron Leader Gwynne was released from duties in December 1945, at the same time as his sister. Back in civvies, one of his first architectural duties was to get himself elected to membership of the Royal Institute of British Architects, the professional body to which the great majority of the country's architects belong. He gained his Licentiate (LRIBA) in May 1946, having furnished the required brief outline of his architectural career and a short recommendation from Denys Lasdun. The additional signatories were his old boss Wells Coates and his friend Ellis Somake, an up-and-coming architect whose designs for the high-class shoe shop chain Dolcis were to be extensively covered in the architectural press during the 1950s and 1960s.[4]

The new peace, Gwynne believed, afforded new opportunities: 'We came back rather bubbling, looking for a Brave New World.' There may have been a country to rebuild, but for many years after the war, austerity and rationing meant that all building efforts were ploughed into basic needs, especially schools and social housing. Lasdun, for example, returned from the army to his old job with Berthold Lubetkin and the Tecton team – he had joined them after Coates closed his office in 1937 – with large housing estates in the pipeline. Although admiring these projects, Gwynne was not interested in working in social architecture. Moreover, he had always been somewhat of a soloist, enjoying his own company and the design control it gave him over a project.

Like most architects setting out in private practice after the war, Gwynne had to scramble about for jobs. As a friend, he helped Lasdun fit out his new flat in Notting Hill. An RAF friend had a few properties, some bombed, requiring repair and small services like bathrooms, and Gwynne felt himself lucky to work on these. Post-war austerity made the situation all 'frightfully shoddy', he recalled, with having to 'make do' with few materials and a scarcity of good craftspeople.

But better jobs slowly began to trickle in. Through Coates's contacts, Gwynne landed his first prominent, if relatively modest, commission in 1949, creating the EMG Handmade Gramophones shop in Newman Street, off London's Oxford Street. A well-known destination for record collectors, the shop housed 17,000 vinyl discs which Gwynne arranged behind the serving staff on shelves attached to a mahogany-lined wall. To prevent the wall collapsing beneath such a great weight of stock, Gwynne used an I-beam girder made in a structural plastic with the trade name of Holoplast, then a novel material. Likewise, customers to this stylish shop were served at a jazzy zigzagging counter faced with Formica, the melamine laminate that

EMG Handmade Gramophones Shop in London's West End, 1949

would soon flood the mass building market and become a staple of modern interior surfaces.[5]

The job with EMG led, three years later, to another gramophone shop, Supreme Radio in the north London suburb of Edmonton, one selling, besides radios, the luxury product everyone wanted by 1952, televisions. The expansive windows afforded the passer-by a clear view of the many sets on display within. As both table radios and televisions were small, boxy and had fronts rather similar in appearance, Gwynne created adjustable shelves arranged on a mahogany wall so that each set stood out on its own.[6]

Supreme Radio shop, Edmonton, London, 1952

All the fitments for Supreme Radio were carried out by his old friend and builder, Leslie Bilsby, now living in Blackheath, south-east London, with his wife and two young daughters.[7] Bilsby was on the road to becoming a successful builder-developer, especially in his role as the very hands-on director for Span Developments Ltd. For over 30 years beginning in 1957, he

115 Blackheath Park, London, photographed by Henk Snoek

transformed the private Cator Estate, a largely Regency development of wide avenues and imposing houses where he lived, with several dozen of Span's popular modern estates of middle-class flats and terraces designed by the architect Eric Lyons.[8]

In 1949, Bilsby asked Gwynne to convert 115 Blackheath Park, the bombed-out shell of a Victorian house at the termination of the Cator Estate's grandest avenue, into his family home. At this period, new private houses were restricted to no more than 900 square feet, but war-damaged dwellings could be rebuilt to their former size, thus allowing for the creation of a substantial two-storey modern villa of 2,800 square feet on the old footprint (see p. 141). Gwynne retained the façade's original tripartite arrangement of windows, accentuating the principal front with angled timber columns and a slatted first-floor balcony to dapple the light within. Covered in slate-coloured asbestos sheets, the distinctive roof was shaped in a curved roll inspired by those used on the popular prefabricated bungalows designed by Gwynne's former colleagues Rodney Thomas and Edric Neel at Arcon; there were even several rows of these temporary shelters with their unique roofs a few minutes' walk away, on the heath.

As with The Homewood and all Gwynne's later houses, the staircase and the dining room were given special treatment. At 115 Blackheath Park, the teak treads of the stairs appeared to float, each suspended on a steel rod fixed to the ceiling. The kitchen contained an elongated bespoke centre island counter, another recurring fixture of almost all his future kitchen

Above: Gwynne's gouache design drawing for the kitchen, 115 Blackheath Park, 1949.
Top right: Dining room. **Bottom right:** Entrance hall

designs. The servery partition to the dining room echoed the slope of the house façade. Light, colourful and cheery, Bilsby's house did not receive coverage in the building press until 1955, when it still looked ultracontemporary after six years.[9]

Experimental curves, especially in the form of concave roof profiles, proved a fascination for Gwynne. In a conjectural but buildable design for a bungalow with a shallow curved roof published in *Ideal Home and Gardening* magazine in 1954, the exterior treatment resembled a hybrid of an Arcon prefab and an aeroplane hangar, a building type very familiar to this former air officer.[10] At 1,500 square feet, the revised maximum new house size allowed for the time, his quantity surveyor Cyril Sweett priced the project at £3,000. Gwynne was aiming for the affluent end of the market. (see p. 135)

The peculiar roof design for the *Ideal Home* house was also related to an arched timber ceiling that Gwynne was working on at the same time: a new music studio adjoining a large Georgian mansion in Highgate. Both

THE WAR AND MID-CENTURY MODERN, 1940–59

beautiful and practical, the studio's bowed ceiling was dramatic and acoustically superb. Measuring 39 by 21 feet, it was one of Gwynne's finest small interiors, spacious and refined, with a large central space comfortably occupied by a pair of grand pianos, the space framed by a pair of side compartments, one for a stylish seating area focused on a fireplace, the other an office on a raised platform. Gwynne had the four narrow steel columns supporting the suspended timber roof covered in fawn leather, the soft surface, he believed, helping to diffuse the sound.

Gwynne linked the studio to the house with a loggia and courtyard, an area large enough for his clients, the world-celebrated classical pianist Sir Clifford Curzon and his wife, the American harpsichordist Lucille, to host outdoor entertainments. The Curzons collected Impressionist paintings, several of which hung in the studio; Gwynne had met them through 'a German friend', probably Curzon's fine-art dealer, Peter Claas.

The Curzon studio received an 'at home' spread in *House and Garden*, the journalist enthusing: 'Decorated in the muted browns of Japanese grass paper and natural woods, the room has a quiet masculine atmosphere with the ceiling giving it a quality of movement in sympathy with the curved forms of the pianos and of the highly decorative horn gramophone'.[11]

In 1958, Gwynne designed another interesting ceiling for a music room, an addition to a substantial Victorian house a few miles along the Portsmouth Road from The Homewood towards Cobham. Its fibrous plaster ceiling was shaped like billowing Gothic vaults, as if this elegant room were a modern chapel. Casually arranged with a grand piano and a seating area around a fireplace, its walls were hung with the owner's old masters, picked out in concealed lighting.

While he was designing Bilsby's Blackheath house, Gwynne scored a notable and very public success with his Crescent Restaurant, so named after its sweeping shape, built for the 1951 Festival Pleasure Gardens in Battersea Park. The commission was a form of consolation prize after Gwynne had entered a competition for a restaurant planned for the Festival's South Bank site. His tented structure was probably 'a bit too jolly' for its neighbours, he later admitted. But it appealed to Hugh Casson, the Festival's Director of Architecture, who recommended Gwynne to James Gardner, the chief designer for the Battersea site. Gwynne's temporary structure proved to be the architect's stepping-stone to further commissions through his connection with Charles Forte (1908–2007), who had acquired the concession to run The Crescent and was on the brink of becoming Britain's 'King of Catering'.

The Festival Gardens were modelled on the famous historic London pleasure gardens of Vauxhall, Ranelagh and Cremorne, which had once stood near the Battersea Park site. There were fountains and flower gardens, dance

THE WAR AND MID-CENTURY MODERN, 1940–59

View through music room for Sir Clifford Curzon to the raised study, Highgate, London, 1955

Music room, Chestnut Lodge, Cobham, Surrey, 1958. The arched plaster ceiling stands free of the walls for indirect lighting on the paintings

pavilions and theatres, fun-fair rides and even a small zoo, with restaurants, bars and beer gardens aplenty. The semicircular form of Gwynne's restaurant enclosed its western end. Like many of the temporary structures on the site, it was a canvas tent, large (reputedly the largest tented restaurant in Europe at the time) and structurally innovative owing to the contribution of the brilliant structural engineer Felix Samuely. Stretching 400 feet from tip to tip, a single open-space interior with no internal upright supports, it held 600 diners. The canvas of the tent was suspended from an exposed concrete frame, with a ring of 26 giant tilted poles cantilevering out at the front, pulling the tent in place, anchored by guy wires into the earth. Flower planters masked the wires at ground level, which some critics thought clever and others a sham.

Metal chandeliers with swirling arms and petal lamps hung from the internal concrete beams, and in keeping with the Regency period theme of the Festival Gardens, surfaces were colourfully striped, the masts wrapped in a blue and white material. Zigzagging ropes patterned the walls, noticeably around the 12 semicircular pavilions for outdoor tables which protruded between the poles like medieval tents, stretching across the whole frontage. The exterior was painted in the colours of the spectrum, from yellow at one end to purple at the other.[12] There were mirrored spheres in the form of revolving circular bouquets of miniature flowers suspended around the outside curve, lit by hidden lights, throwing a glittering ballroom radiance across the façade and forecourt. The *Architect and Building News* perceptively picked up on the mix of modernity and frivolity, saying that it was a structure 'in which members of MARS and Maharajahs will be equally at home'.[13]

As the 1950s progressed, Gwynne gained a series of commissions for fine interiors that found their way into the pages of the building and design journals. Only one client hated his work so much that he refused to move in. The remodelling of Peter Claas's flat in Upper Brook Street, Mayfair, in 1950 had included a parrot cage in the Festival style, made of aluminium with concealed lighting and decorated with circular wooden balls like diagrams of molecular structures. The parrot 'loathed it', Gwynne remembered with a chuckle, 'and was foul mouthed'.

Fortunately, humans were more impressed with Gwynne's work. In 1952, nearly a decade and a half after Cyril Sweett had acted as quantity surveyor on The Homewood, Gwynne redesigned his house in Notting Hill Gate. For wallpapers, even Sanderson's fell far below Gwynne's exacting standards so that he had one handmade to get the preferred width of 'Regency stripe'. For the drawing room, Gwynne fashioned a crate-sized music cabinet, covered in brown leather, upon which the client scattered magazines and books, clearing them away for musical evenings when the recently introduced 33 1/3 rpm records were played on the twin turntables. Gwynne's connections

THE WAR AND MID-CENTURY MODERN, 1940–59

Crescent Restaurant, 1951 Festival of Britain, Festival Pleasure Gardens, Battersea, London, photographed by H L Wainwright, 1951. Tented dining pavilions ring the front of the 600-seat temporary restaurant

A parrot cage in the Festival of Britain style, 1950. The parrot refused to move in

at EMG Gramophones came in useful for such little projects and he had a similar gramophone made for himself.

Sweett and Gwynne reunited one final time, in 1958, when Gwynne designed the engineer's new London offices in Bedford Row, Holborn. Gwynne called the layout 'open plan', but it was in fact a series of spaces separated by partitions. These little offices divided by screens – stud post and plywood surfaces, doors and large glazing – were so simple that Gwynne's detailed drawings in the glossy pages of the Architectural Design look like instructions for elegant sheds. Yet the effect was crisp and modern. Luxury was saved for Sweett's private office, where behind an undulating outer wall of white glass mosaic tiles, the large corner suite had walls covered in grey Japanese grass wallpaper and a ceiling in a new vinyl synthetic imitation leathercloth called 'Vynide'.[14]

Sweett had also facilitated Gwynne's third shop commission in 1953, introducing him to Charles Clore, the financier and retail and property magnate, who had recently acquired Freeman, Hardy and Willis, a major shoe chain with shops in almost every major British high street. Clore wanted 'a new look' and gave Gwynne a free hand, resulting in a great success and enormous failure in equal measure.

Custom-made and sophisticated, the shop had a bright welcoming interior lit like new modern offices by a ceiling lined with Perspex panels, and showcases displaying shoes in glass boxes like ornaments. The problem, as Gwynne freely admitted, was the building's location at the entrance to the bazaar of open market stalls in the heart of the very busy working-class area of Catford in south-east London. This elegant shoe shop which, as he said, would have been suitable for Bond Street, looked like Cinderella's glass slipper waiting for a Prince Charming who never came. It closed quickly and was replaced. But Clore was pleased, for seeing the shop illustrated in the pages of The Director magazine made it a success in his eyes, worth what he had spent. And photographs of the project made the pages of Architect and Building News, supplemented by Gwynne's fine set of exploded axonometrics showing assembly drawings, probably made to show Clore how the design could be rolled out quickly and efficiently in other locations.[15]

Gwynne liked and admired Sweett, but found that he 'procrastinated'.[16] Bilsby introduced him to another quantity surveyor, Kenneth Monk of Monk and Dunstone. Gwynne and Monk saw eye to eye immediately; over two decades they were partners in speculative houses and several overseas projects. One of their first jobs together, in about 1960, was the remodelling of the Monk and Dunstone offices, a process repeated some years later at a new location.

Another of Gwynne's commercial jobs from the mid-1950s afforded a piece of street theatre. Through the large pavement windows of the London

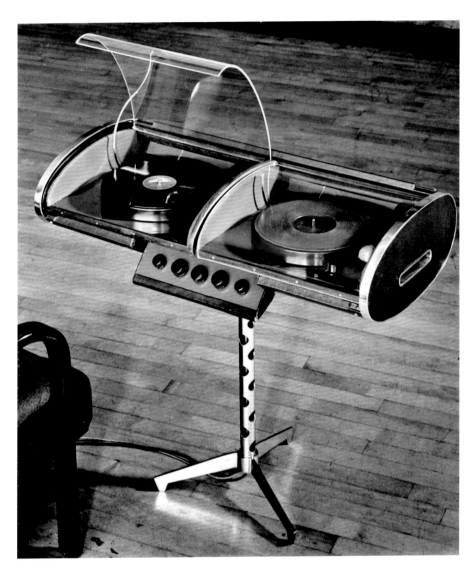

Dual turntable gramophone designed by Gwynne for his own use, 1952

Press Exchange, an advertising agency in St Martin's Lane in the West End, Gwynne displayed a room with a working computer. In those days, computers were enormous pieces of machinery, requiring him to raise the whole space up to get the mass of cabling beneath.

Other small engagements kept him going during the 1950s. Like many designers of his generation, he found himself creating exhibition stands for the building trade as it geared up for post-war production. In 1953,

Shoe shop for Freeman, Hardy and Willis, Catford, London, photographed by Edgar Hyman, 1953

for example, he fashioned a casual living room atmosphere for the Royal Institute of Chartered Surveyors' stand at the Building Exhibition at London's Olympia centre.[17]

And like most architects, Gwynne entered competitions. The Crescent Restaurant had been a success, but his entry for a National Gallery extension in 1958–9 turned out to be a publicity stunt by the *Sunday Times*, and fell flat. Similarly, his beautiful gouache drawings for a competition in 1957 held by the Canadian Wood Association for designs for a timber house were not placed, but with their stylish interiors and exterior forms based upon the Bilsby house, they perfectly illustrated Gwynne's small house ideal.

In 1955 came two restaurants. One was the Butterwalk Restaurant and Coffee Bar in Dartmouth, Devon, a project within a historic fabric that showed a sensitive blend of new with old. With highly carved exteriors, 10 The Butterwalk is one in a row of crooked timber-framed merchant houses dating from about 1640 that had been recently restored following war damage. The first-floor interior drips with ornamental plaster and carved decoration, the ceiling is highly patterned, and above the stone fireplace a large overmantel shows a crowded scene of Jesus and the Apostles on the day of Pentecost. This space was 'the good class restaurant', so Gwynne designed upmarket furniture such as crescent-shaped banquettes and a matching terrazzo and stone buffet.[18] More curious and surreal were the life-size sculpted hands gripping multilight floor lamps and used to display the menu at the entrance. Seating in the ground-floor coffee bar took the form of leather pad cushions placed on benches and affixed to the wall as backs – a practice that Gwynne came to use on his residential patios. The crescent-shaped bar sported a very large and trendy espresso machine.

The other restaurant of 1955 was more elegant, as befitted a hip hangout serving the first wave of affluent bohemians cultivating London's Chelsea. The Ox on the Roof Restaurant in King's Road had opened in 1949 and gained a fine reputation, its interior by the architect Michael Rachlis, who had specialised in restaurant design in pre-war Berlin. Gwynne had discovered the restaurant when he strayed over the river while working on the Crescent Restaurant and befriended its Austrian husband and English wife owners. The couple asked him to create a dining room on the first floor. Here diners found themselves seated upon curving banquettes in yellow and deep-blue upholstery, bathed in red light like a nightclub, beneath a ceiling plastered in geometrically patterned plaster, and surrounded by walls hung with wonderful tapestries, curtains and an oil painting by Jean Lurçat. One critic excitedly wrote of the Japanese food, including the novelty of stir-fry at the table. A sure sign of its success, he wrote, was that 'the place was full of youth and beauty'.[19]

Finally, in 1958, Gwynne received his first post-war house commission – he had not considered Bilsby's rebuild to be a new building. Bespoke houses henceforth cemented his architectural reputation. In almost all cases over the next 25 years, his closest associates were Bilsby as builder and developer and Monk as quantity surveyor. The new commission came about through an old Sandroyd school friend, Hugh Latimer, now a well-known film actor, who introduced Gwynne to Jack Hawkins, who had been Latimer's commanding officer in the war. Hawkins was one of the stars of *The Bridge on the River Kwai*, which won the Academy Award for best film in 1958, just as Gwynne was completing the house for Hawkins' mother-in-law, Mrs Beadle. The outcome made for an excellent spread in *Ideal Home*, with photographs of the famous Jack Hawkins, his wife, daughter and Mrs Beadle enjoying their 'strikingly modern house'.[20]

Externally, the two-storey house in a quiet corner of Bournemouth had much in common with Bilsby's: the roof pitch was similar and, most noticeably, the front had the same tripartite composition marked by posts on the ground floor and a central balcony flanked by bedrooms on the upper.

PATRICK GWYNNE

THE WAR AND MID-CENTURY MODERN, 1940–59

Ox on the Roof Restaurant, Chelsea, London, 1955

A curved wall faced in Purbeck stone and front entrance behind the posts broke the façade's linearity and foreshadowed the serpentine brick walls that would become a trademark of many of Gwynne's later houses.

As Mrs Beadle was a semi-invalid, she lived on the ground floor with the master bedroom, living room and kitchen arranged in an L-shape around a walled courtyard (see p. 141). As an indication of her commitment to the modern, or more probably at Gwynne's insistence, she replaced all her old furniture with stylish new pieces. And with a dishwasher, electric waste-disposal and automatic central heating, *Ideal Home* was able to chide its more traditional readers by saying 'it is well to recognise that the elderly can often adapt themselves to contemporary surroundings and appreciate the advantages of labour-saving equipment'.

Butterwalk Restaurant and Café, Dartmouth, Devon, 1955, built within an historic 1640 plastered interior

PATRICK GWYNNE

The actor Jack Hawkins commissioned this Bournemouth house from Gwynne for his mother-in-law, 1958

The glass-walled kitchen looking into the courtyard of the Hawkins house

Gwynne's friendship with Monk led to their first venture together during 1959–60. Monk acted as developer in the construction of Gwynne's design for four speculative houses grouped neatly around a central forecourt on a landscaped two-acre plot in Coombe Hill Road, Kingston upon Thames. 'This was an unusual experiment', wrote Alice Hope in 1963, in that buyers in the 'higher income groups' preferred custom-made over spec houses, and that Gwynne's development offered 'something in the way of bait that was rather special'.[21]

Gwynne described these two-storey flat-roofed houses as simple because the interiors were not decked out in his usual costly built-in furniture. They were, however, interestingly planned and well appointed. All four had the same spacious rectangular plan offset by the sweeping serpentine curves of the garden walls that linked the houses and their garages (see p. 141). A central staircase in each house, lit by a skylight, also housed the downpipes and flue so that the external lines were pristine; as Dr Salmon, one of Gwynne's clients at the time, remarked, 'Patrick couldn't stand the sight of a pipe', and none of his buildings were spoiled by them. Each house was faced in different coloured concrete brick and internally colour was added gently so as not to scare prospective buyers, with tiling in kitchens in primrose and bathrooms in blue and pink. Named Fairoaks, Mulberry, Woodlands and Junipers, all but one of the quartet have been demolished, and the survivor has had a pitched roof added.

In 1959, *Ideal Home* magazine covered Gwynne's second client-based house in an article with a title that poetically summed up the aesthetic he was pursuing: 'The Line of Beauty'.[22] The phrase, borrowed from the painter William Hogarth, refers to the curving s-shape line of a form that finds beauty, grace and even sensuality in art.

The Firs was the first of three houses close by to each other that Gwynne built just north of Hampstead Heath, London. All the clients were German Jewish émigrés, people that Gwynne believed were 'without doubt' more receptive to modernism. Otto Edler, an engineer, had been living in Hampstead Garden Suburb with his wife Marion and their two children when Bilsby made the introduction. The new house that Gwynne designed for them at 24 Spaniards End was the first of his buildings with a ground plan based candidly upon the curve, the side walls adopting a gentle s-bend, tapering from the wide garden front to the smaller rear wall (see p. 141). The arrangement of the front echoed his houses of the previous decade, a tripartite composition over two storeys, emphasised by a vertical quartet of non-load-bearing metal poles, a small ornamental pool beneath the central bow window playfully throwing patterns of light within.

The interior was comfortable and well appointed. Concealing was as important as revealing. The semicircular staircase, encased in thin vertical

Serpentine garden walls linked the four speculative houses at Coombe Hill, Kingston upon Thames, that Gwynne designed for his client and friend the quantity surveyor Kenneth Monk, 1960, photographed by H L Wainwright

boarding, has open risers, each tread illuminated by hidden lighting, lines of beauty reinforced by a sinuous white tubular steel handrail. (*see* p. x) The three rooms overlooking the garden – dining room, living room and study – are a free-flowing space that can be divided off by recessed sliding partitions. A dappled grey wall of marble showcases the fireplace while also camouflaging the doors of the compartment for a turntable that rotates the television between the living and dining rooms. Gwynne used his favourite Japanese grass paper for the walls and designed most of the fittings and furniture, including the lighting. There was built-in furniture in all the rooms, as well as free-standing sofas with an integrated record player in the living area. Curtain rails were cleverly concealed throughout the house by curling the ceiling cove over them. The modern setting was enhanced by the Edler's small but fine collection of works by Cezanne, Soutine and Picasso.

Gwynne returned to The Firs 40 years later, in 1999, at the invitation of its new owners, William Sargent and Sharon Reed, who asked his opinion on refurbishment and making changes. Arriving in his Cambridge-blue v8 Vantage Aston Martin, 'he wandered around touching everything, looking into cupboards, smiling and walking on', the couple recalled. 'It was very moving, like watching a reunion of old friends.'[23] Always contemporary, never nostalgic or historicist, Gwynne advised them to upgrade, pointing

THE WAR AND MID-CENTURY MODERN, 1940–59

The Edlers on the terrace of The Firs, 2 Spaniards End, Hampstead, London, 1959

out that in post-war Britain paint colours were limited and technology basic. Nevertheless, the couple were sensitive with their amendments, most notably reinstating the exterior metal poles which had been removed and employing an architect noted for modern restoration, John Allan of Avanti Architects, to add a small studio at the rear. Gwynne gave his blessing.

The clients of Gwynne's second Hampstead house were Max and Anne Bruh, the owners of Frank Usher, a successful fashion house. Having purchased part of the garden of a large house located at 4 Beechworth Close overlooking West Heath, and rejecting the designs of one architect, a friend told them about The Firs. Impressed, they contacted Gwynne, who invited them to The Homewood, which always captivated prospective clients, and quickly convinced them with a spacious design for their family of four.

Completed in 1961 to a generous budget, the Bruh house is what Gwynne called 'pavilion-like': a plan of two layered rectangles with the upper level containing the bedrooms being smaller than the larger ground-floor living spaces (see p. 142).[24] The exterior is a composition in light and dark: the ground storey is of inky-brown brick with black metal window and door surrounds, while the upper floor with dark glass panels set beneath the windows was rendered in white cement called Mineralite, which glittered with glass particles. The whole house is edged in the thick black lines of the

Entrance to The Firs. The tiles of the wall are terracotta red and the floor in mottled grey-green

exposed concrete construction that had been coated in a coloured aggregate with the delightful name of Glamorock.

The interior is one of Gwynne's richest and most restrained, all worked out right down to the free-standing furniture, the architect taking his clients along to Heal's, the most fashionable furnishing shop in London, to guide their selection, or rather, as was his wont, to gently dictate his tastes. In the

THE WAR AND MID-CENTURY MODERN, 1940–59

The Edlers entertain at The Firs, captured in a 1959 article about their new house in *Ideal Home and Gardening*

centre of the house stands another of Gwynne's fine staircases, in terrazzo, continuing the exterior black and white theme with white treads and black risers. At his suggestion, the black lacquered sideboard was painted in gold Chinese decoration by the artist Peter Thompson, the oriental refrain developed in the living room with red silk seat coverings and buff silk wallpaper. The kitchen is especially well kitted out, with an expanse of orange tilework – Gwynne increasingly falling under the spell of zones of coloured tiles – as well as one of his signature kitchen islands, chocked with drawers and a fitted marble pastry board. On the mottled-white-tiled wall is a servants' bell panel incorporating a clock and intercom, custom designed in stainless steel. The already finely treed garden was manicured under Gwynne's direction, with his own gardener, Mr Baldwin, laying out the bedding and new planting.

In 1963, Michael and José Manser gave 4 Beechworth Close a glowing review in the pages of the short-lived magazine *Home*, writing that 'Max and Anne Bruh's house has the quality and sophistication that only supreme professionalism can give'.[25] The Mansers' appreciation of Gwynne's architecture would become instrumental many decades later in the saving of The Homewood by the National Trust.

PATRICK GWYNNE

Bruh House, Hampstead, London, completed in 1961

With his third Hampstead house, Gwynne returned to his interest in the sinuous line. Built in 1963 next door to the Bruh's, at 3 Beechworth Close, on a small plot formerly occupied by a tennis court, Mr and Mrs Hornung's new house was a sculpted version of Gwynne's four speculative houses in Coombe Hill, similar in plan but shaped with rounded corners, in a 'tub-like form', said Gwynne (see p. 142). The interior was fairly plain compared to the other Hampstead houses, but nevertheless had a fine central staircase, panelling, colourful tiling and sliding screens for room dividers. With the curve of its brick exterior and boundary walls, it was a contrast to the black and white Bruh house, which pleased Mrs Bruh as she had made it clear to Gwynne that she did not want a smaller version of her house immediately adjacent.

As Gwynne was completing the first of the Hampstead houses, he embarked on another of his important houses, Past Field, whose gentle

The divider between the sunken living room and dining room of the Bruh House, built 1961

v-shape plan made the clients, physician Dr Anthony (Tony) Salmon and his wife Elizabeth (Liz, née Humphries), jokingly refer to their home as 'the boomerang' (see p. 142). The Salmons were a thoroughly modern couple: Liz, a professional singer and pianist, had appeared in the British premier of the hit musical *Guys and Dolls* and they loved new architecture. She had first met Gwynne when she dropped around to The Homewood to rehearse with pianist and composer Geoffrey Rand, Gwynne's live-in friend at the time. She returned home exclaiming 'I've been to an extraordinary house, marvellous house'.[26] So when in 1957 a grateful client gave the Salmons a beautiful plot of land at the brow of a hill in Henley-on-Thames, Oxfordshire, they asked Gwynne round to see it; he arrived stylishly, as always, in yet another new sports car. Gwynne sat with the couple and made a few sketches in coloured pencil showing variant ideas, a favourite technique he had for impressing clients. The Salmons were hooked and exclaimed, 'God, that's perfect!' Architect and clients instantly hit it off and would remain lifelong friends, going to the opera at Glyndebourne and holidaying together, including a visit to Gwynne's ancestral Welsh home.

The curve of the Henley house enfolds the landscape, all the principal rooms opening onto the garden and panoramic view. The kink in the v of the plan incorporates the all-glass rear and garden entrances, separating the living areas on one side from the sleeping quarters on the other, a layout Gwynne used in many of his houses. The living area was large enough for relaxed seating around a fireplace and for one grand piano at first and eventually two, since both the Salmons played. The walls are of exposed brick – Uxbridge flettons: dark purple on the living side, lavender in the bedrooms. Dining rooms and bathrooms are timber panelled, and rich hardwoods used for built-in fixtures. The roof is another of the architect's curved monopitch essays, a soft angular s-shape, dramatically overhanging the garden terrace by seven feet and angled down to the rear, giving the ceilings of the interior rooms a graceful movement.

Work began on the house in March 1959 and took nine months to complete. During construction, Gwynne, being his usual meticulous self, noticed that the prescribed 3-inch steel poles holding up the roof were nearly 3½ inches. The managing director of the local contracting firm, Mr Walden, who was then president of the Association of House Builders, got an earful from Gwynne for making them 'fat'. Walden said that he had never been spoken to like that before, to which Gwynne dryly replied, 'Well, that's a pity'. The contractor had to shore up the whole roof and replace the poles to the given specification.[27]

The house was planned to take extensions, so in 1966 the Salmons had Gwynne return to add a large master bedroom at one end and a new kitchen and covered patio at the other. A keen amateur carpenter, Dr

THE WAR AND MID-CENTURY MODERN, 1940–59

Past Field, Henley-on-Thames, Oxfordshire, built in 1960 with 1966 additions at both ends

The living room of Past Field with its sloping ceiling

Salmon used Gwynne's sketches to build some of the units himself, such as the timber-panelled wall with a serving hatch and alcoves in the new dining room, formerly the old kitchen, and a great octagonal window in the new kitchen.

As Gwynne was dealing with the completion of the last of his Hampstead jobs, he obtained the commission for what would be the largest of all his houses, one just slightly bigger than The Homewood. Witley Park, designed near Godalming, Surrey, for Gerald Bentall, is a true English country house in the traditional sense: imposing, made for entertaining and set on a vast estate. But it was more convenient and comfortable, as Mark Girouard noted in *Country Life* on its completion in 1962: 'it is a country house adapted to present-day conditions, scaled down in size and capable of being run with the help of a single living-in couple and a daily help'.[28] Because all the main living spaces were at first-floor level, Gwynne joked that it was just 'a bungalow raised up on columns'.

Gwynne's invitation for the prospective client to visit and, hopefully, be charmed by The Homewood not only clinched the deal, but proved the catalyst for Witley Park's design. Bentall saw the advantage of raised living spaces with large windows as perfect for appreciating the expansive views over his estate. Moreover, as the entrepreneurial and forward-thinking owner of the large Bentall's department store in Kingston upon Thames, Surrey, he appreciated Gwynne's modern style and fondness for technical gadgetry.

The Witley Park estate came with quite an architectural history. An enormous neo-Tudor house from the 1890s had been gutted by fire in 1952, and by 1960 there remained only gardens and parterres overlooking an artificial lake containing one of the most fabulous of Victorian follies, an iron and glass billiards room beneath its waters. Gwynne wanted the new house on the site of the old, but Bentall insisted upon another location some distance away, on a slight rise, nestled near a small copse of trees to the north and with uninterrupted views to the South Downs.

There was no doubt that the exterior of Witley Park was the toughest looking of Gwynne's houses, one that could stylistically be labelled Brutalist. The ground floor is of reinforced concrete with four massive square piers around the terrace, all clad in roughly hewn blocks of golden Hornton stone to give a warmer and more traditional feel. The taller, overhanging upper storey dominates, and is steel framed on a concrete floor plate. Great concrete cladding panels of Derbyshire spar – a cream, white and grey aggregate – were lifted into place and hung on inset steel hooks, an operation that Gwynne filmed on his home cinecamera.

Witley Park marked the first time that Gwynne based the plan of one of his buildings on deliberate geometric forms, two- and three-dimensional arrangements of space that were usually symmetrical, a modification of

THE WAR AND MID-CENTURY MODERN, 1940-59

Witley Park, near Godalming, Surrey, for Gerald Bentall, was photographed by H L Wainwright for the *Architectural Review* and *Country Life*, 1962

the modular system he had used with The Homewood (*see* p. 142). The arrangement of Witley Park is based upon the hexagon. The shape is most apparent in the six-sided external columns and planting beds of the patio. But the v-shaped plan too, although not a strict grouping of hexagons, is a series of 120-degree angles (a hexagon being 6 × 120 degrees). Gwynne set enormous windows at almost all of the angles, thus providing split panoramic views.

The interior was bespoke, restrained luxury with, as the thick sales catalogue produced in 1973 upon Bentall's death stressed, 'every modern "gadget of the time"'.[29] The great hexagon at the west end of the house was shared between the living room – so large that the grand piano seemed incidental – and a sizeable dining room. These main spaces were divided by sliding aluminium doors painted by Peter Thompson. There was also one of Gwynne's signature fireplace walls, clad in Austrian elm with illuminated display recesses, integral television and phonograph cabinets, speakers, a movie projector and retractable screen, a revolving bar to the kitchen passageway, refrigerator, telephone and directory cupboards, and concealed spotlights to flood the concave ceiling of the room. All the louvred blinds, throughout the house and to the sliding glazed roof of the sunroom, operated electrically. Gwynne designed light fittings and long built-in banquettes for lounging beneath the great windows. Furniture, wardrobes, sideboards and shelving in master and guest suites, staff flat and offices for Bentall and his secretary were all designed by Gwynne with the exception of the chairs, although he did create the double sofa in the living area. The fittings were 'all beautifully made', said the architect, who always held good craftspeople in high regard. The bathrooms with their colourful tiles and the kitchen were, as to be expected, well appointed, and lights automatically came on when doors were opened to the wine cellar and deep-freeze. The three-car garage, separated from the house, was heated.

A principal focus of Witley Park was the entrance hall staircase. Gwynne was rightly proud of it. If ever a staircase was said to float, this is it. Beautifully contoured white terrazzo treads, independent of each other, the bottom one not even touching the floor, the whole staircase appears not to join the wall since it is cantilevered from beneath by imperceptible steel tubes with lighting for each step. Hovering over the stairs with no balusters or supports, the massive teak handrail, a line of beauty similar to the one in the Bruh house, had a steel core fixed at the top landing. Gwynne felt the 'heavy staircase ... suited the client; Bentall was a big man, a bit dour'.

A few months after moving into Witley Park, Bentall suffered a stroke. He recovered, but this necessitated a six-passenger lift. At the time, Gwynne also was undertaking the redesign of Bentall's office in his Kingston department store that entailed the complete removal of the original 1930s interior.

For a brief period after Gerald Bentall's death in 1971, Witley Park came into the hands of an owner who barely made use of it, and then it was sold to the communications industrialist Sir Raymond Brown. A keen horse lover, polo player and golfer, Brown used the 1,400-acre estate for shooting and keeping prize-winning Hereford cattle. Lady Carol Brown, a force in her own right, asked Gwynne back to make changes. These were alterations which Gwynne did not wish to make, but in Lady Brown he met his match; the job was a rare instance of him not walking away when not getting his own way. Moreover, as he admitted, it was better that he made the changes than someone else. This exercise in damage limitation included altering the fireplace wall by removing panelling and recesses for shelving to take books. The sliding doors with Peter Thompson's artwork were put into store in the garage and replaced with swing doors between the living and dining rooms, which Lady Brown felt more appropriate when giving dinner parties.

Gwynne and Lady Brown remained friends after Sir Raymond's death in 1991 as she continued to run Witley Park house and estate. A decade or so later, she sold the property to Gary Steele, an American cyber-security guru who abandoned Gwynne's house for a new neo-Georgian mansion on the site of the former Victorian house overlooking the lake, ironic in the light of Girouard's *Country Life* article on Gwynne's house four decades previously that had been optimistically titled 'A Change from Neo-Georgian'.

THE WAR AND MID-CENTURY MODERN, 1940–59

The living room of Witley Park with its undulating wall of Austrian elm containing the fireplace and concealing a large entertainment centre

Entrance hall with its staircase of floating stairs and handrail, Witley Park

5 The art of living 1960–84

In April 1963, Charles Forte, the restaurateur behind Gwynne's 1951 Crescent Restaurant, resurfaced in Patrick Gwynne's career. Now a household name as the leading caterer in the country, he owned extensive chains like Little Chef, Happy Eater and Travelodge, had bought the prestigious Café Royal in Regent Street and taken on the country's first motor service area at Newport Pagnell in 1959. Forte secured a contract from the Royal Parks of London and invited six architectural practices, including Gwynne, to submit ideas for a pair of restaurant buildings in Hyde Park, both overlooking the waters of the Serpentine. The largest of the two venues would become the Serpentine Restaurant, sited near the bridge; the smaller Dell Restaurant was at its eastern tip.

Gwynne won the commission by presenting a printed volume of design concepts, illustrated by his coloured-up drawings, as well as a set of collages of the proposed structures made by photographing models and then superimposing them onto a photograph of the park. The Serpentine Restaurant was composed of hexagonal-shaped 'umbrellas', as Gwynne called them, in concrete, largely glassed in (*see* p. 144). And, as the park lacked a conservatory, he integrated plants as a feature. But in winning, he found himself 'very much fussed' by meetings with Forte's company and the Ministry of Public Building and Works which managed structures in the Royal Parks, with 'everybody saying what should be done' – but which 'I wasn't going to do'. To get away from the bickering, he went on holiday to Amalfi; unable to sleep during a thunderstorm, he polished off the final design for the Serpentine Restaurant. Returning to his office, he hired John Grey as his assistant architect who acted as middleman, imposing Gwynne's will on any troublemakers. Kenneth Monk, Gwynne's quantity surveyor, recommended GM Associates as executive architects who admirably kept the 'very aggressive' builders Sir Robert McAlpine at bay. Construction began in October 1963 and proceeded rapidly, with a grand opening on Whit Monday, 18 May 1964. Forte gave a speech praising himself, without mentioning his architect, said an irritated Gwynne.

Theatre Royal, York. Gwynne's extension and interior refit opened in 1967

PATRICK GWYNNE

Serpentine Restaurant, Hyde Park, London, photographed by John Donat, 1964

The bar of the Serpentine Restaurant, 1964

THE ART OF LIVING 1960–84

The Serpentine Restaurant was demolished in 1990

The building was an instant success, a geometric ornament as well as a fun dining and drinking destination in London's most famous park. There was a large restaurant and cocktail bar in one of the two pavilions and a self-service cafeteria and bar in the other. Strolling through the park, visitors were greeted by this most remarkable structure, raised high on colossal sloping concrete piers topped by a striking cluster of six tall hexagonal 'pods'. These spires doubled as conservatories with large plants, blinds to the sunny side, extractor fans at the top and heating below. The pods encircled a hexagonal glass room with angled walls and no fewer than six entrances: this was the bar, where patrons could raise a pint while enjoying elevated views through the treetops and over the lake. Across a small open terrace, paved with triangular concrete tiles, was the larger of the two pavilions, boasting the novelty of a chef cooking over an open-to-view charcoal grill. This pavilion was set beneath a vaulted forest of blossoming pillars, the architect's 'umbrellas'. 'It's a lovely concrete form', said Gwynne of the mushroom-topped columns, 'a post with a lid on top, and you simply shape it'.

75

At first the concession was used only in the summer. Before the second season Gwynne proudly took Denys Lasdun to see it, only to discover that over the winter no one had bothered to maintain the conservatory pods and that all the plants were dead. They were replanted, but never kept up.

'Delightfully bizarre', wrote John Donat in his review of the Serpentine Restaurant in the *Architectural Review*.[1] So successful was the enterprise that Gwynne was asked to extend the restaurant the year after completion. The cellular honeycomb structure made additions easy, and he simply raised a further series of hexagonal units with more concrete mushrooms. Five years later, Forte asked for yet more restaurant space, so in 1971 Gwynne extended the terrace with a low structure lit by triangular-shaped acrylic skylights, in other words, halved hexagons.

The Serpentine was demolished in 1990, the catering lease having run out. There was a small movement to save it, but it was less than 30 years old so therefore ineligible for heritage listing save at a high grade, and it was not then appreciated as having sufficient value. Sherban Cantacuzino of the Royal Fine Art Commission who was also Wells Coates's biographer, together with Gwynne's old friend Michael Manser, now a past president of the RIBA, 'led a campaign', that was reported in *Building Design*. A front-page column of the weekly was accompanied by a photograph of the building, titled 'London Landmark'.[2]

As Gwynne completed the designs for the Serpentine Restaurant's first extension in late 1963, he began the Dell Restaurant – it survives as a listed building. Opened on 12 July 1965, it hovers at the eastern tip of the Serpentine, drifting over the water's edge like a giant water lily. His competition design had proposed a three-storey octagonal stack of mushroom pillars, each floor increasing in size from bottom up, like an inverted wedding cake. Half the lower structure would have been below water level, giving patrons the choice of relaxing overlooking the water or descending into the 'Under-Water Bar' with an aquarium viewing wall.

As built, the Dell has a profile similar to a sunhat with a broad scalloped brim. The proportions and ratios are all about the octagon: the copper roof is octagonal and its central service core springs from the spokes of eight steel beams (*see* p. 144). The building is a galaxy of elements set at 135°angles, the inner congruent of a regular octagon; wonderful views over the Serpentine are seen through a zigzagging wall of glass, and all the terrazzo benches encircling the outside seating area weave in and out over the water at the given angle.

The stylish interior, removed in subsequent refurbishments, had a bar and serving counter around the central service drum, naturally lit by a continuous strip of skylights. The interior was a complete Gwynne creation: precast terrazzo seating with deep-red upholstery, egg-shaped moulded

THE ART OF LIVING 1960–84

The Dell Restaurant, Hyde Park, London, 1965, a smart bar and restaurant

fibreglass tub chairs, ceiling lights with hanging plants, and large peripheral uplighters with small motors and coloured discs swirling light around the building and off the water. The Dell was a smart venue, the chef resplendent in full white uniform and *toque blanche*, the barman in black tie. Prior to its listing, when it was either removed or covered up, there was a large wall mural behind the servery by Stefan Knapp, made of vitreous enamelled steel panels decorated in swirls of gold, silver and copper leaf.

Gwynne's third major project of the 1960s was the renovation and extension of the Theatre Royal in York, an appropriate commission for Gwynne who had friends in the theatre and film world. This job came unexpectedly. In 1965, Donald Bodley, the progressive young director of the Theatre Royal, found himself saddled with a traditional design for a proposed extension to the building, one that Gwynne panned for looking

The Dell Restaurant, at dusk

Victorian Gothic stone meets concrete Brutalism in Gwynne's extension to the Theatre Royal, York, 1967, photographed by Henk Snoek

THE ART OF LIVING 1960–84

Staircase and upper levels with restaurant at the Theatre Royal, York, 1967

like 'a small office block'. That summer, Bodley walked into the Serpentine Restaurant and knew that he had found the right architect.[3] Contacting Gwynne, he very quickly received a basic design that the York Citizens Theatre Trust glowingly approved.

Work for the Theatre Royal involved the refurbishment of the old building and the addition of an extension providing for a large foyer and audience amenities, thus serving as the new principal front of house (see p. 145). York has a venerable history and the site of the theatre lies upon Roman ruins and the remains of a medieval hospital in the heart of the city near the art gallery and minster. A much-loved institution going back to 1744, the theatre had been made over in 1879 by the local city engineer George Styan in what Gwynne, never a lover of Victorian architecture, called 'fairly corny High

Gothic'. But he thought the interior pretty, an Edwardian facelift from 1902 by the highly respected theatre architect Frank A Tugwell of Scarborough.

Gwynne had the exterior cleaned, and the auditorium repainted in matt greens and given new seating; old staircases were removed, and dressing rooms and a green room added. But the real showstopper was his extension: a modest but striking double-storey building dominated by concrete mushroom columns similar to those that Bodley had so appreciated at the Serpentine Restaurant. Like the Dell, the exterior walls of the York building were a series of angled plate-glass windows, using the biggest sheets then available. Nikolaus Pevsner admired how the mushroom 'canopies are like the vaults rising from the central piers of English chapter houses'.[4] Gwynne had acquired the medieval reference by playing up the Gothic features of the old theatre in exposing one of its stone exterior side walls within the new building, its series of pointed arched openings at ground floor now reused as entrances to the auditorium. Access to upper levels is by Gwynne's most operatic staircase, a dramatic and technical achievement consisting of a series of walkways, foyers and services. He was pleased to open two national papers on his 87th birthday in 2000 to find pictures of his York buildings with an admiring commentary after 35 years in use.[5]

In 1970, when Dr Salmon's medical practice group were given the opportunity to build a new surgery and offices, he convinced his colleagues that Gwynne was their architect. The Hart Medical Surgery in Henley is another of Gwynne's fascinating geometrical plans, a semicircular starburst of doctors' suites and treatment rooms radiating from a top-lit central reception and waiting room (*see* p. 145). Gwynne luckily found the three doctors on the committee compliant to his ideas: 'they didn't murmur on anything, they just accepted the whole reasoning I put into the thing'. The doctors' desks were curved to separate them from patients, which worked well except for one doctor who was left-handed, so Gwynne had the desk made in reverse.

The surgery, like Salmon's house, was designed to be extended with further cells on a symmetrical pattern; indeed, later Gwynne was able to add two offices neatly around the reception nucleus. When a small off-side addition was made by another architect, breaking slightly with the pattern, he found it unsympathetic 'in that rather greedy manner people have'.

Forte meanwhile retained Gwynne for a spell of jobs, with only one built: the Burtonwood Motorway Services Area in Forte's growing Motorchef chain, a matching pair of restaurant buildings on either side of the M62 near Warrington, Cheshire. Opened in 1974, Gwynne's buildings were among the most architecturally interesting on the motorway network, with eye-catching silhouettes like a pair of Buddhist stupas topped with jagged-peaked copper roofs.

THE ART OF LIVING 1960–84

Surgery, Henley-on-Thames, photographed by Christine Ottewill, 1970

Similar to the Dell Restaurant, both road pavilions were, as Gwynne declared, 'coaxed into an octagon' (see p. 146). The interior of each required slightly different arrangements. By law, lorry drivers had their own 'transport café' separated from the public with half-price food, while toilets, a shop and kitchens were shared with the other travellers. One pavilion boasted a posh grill restaurant, with the sloping roofs giving height and interest.[6] The spaces were top-lit in daylight by sets of 10-foot-high windows which encircled the roof cone housing the giant water tank, required as a fire precaution. Many of the walls in the public areas were covered in tile mosaics, mostly very colourful.[7]

The Burtonwood buildings were Gwynne's second attempt at a motorway service area. A decade earlier, in 1964, Forte had commissioned a scheme in an attempt to land the concession for Heston on the M4, but another company got the business. Gwynne's design, with a great reinforced concrete roof, like a graceful shell, recalled the innovative work by concrete specialists of the time, like Pier Luigi Nervi in Italy and Mexico's Félix Candela (see p. 144). Burtonwood also spawned one later commission, for a site on

83

The matching Motorchef restaurants at the Burtonwood Motorway Services Area, M62 near Warrington, Cheshire, 1974; only one survives today

the M11 near Chigwell, Essex, not built due to rising costs; its decagonal (ten-sided) plan was reminiscent of an Italian Baroque church complete with radiating aedicules and apse (actually the grill room) (*see* p. 146).

Burtonwood also inspired one of Gwynne's most overlooked buildings, another restaurant in a park setting, in Dubai. The approach for the project came from a Pakistani businessman who had admired the Hyde Park restaurants and was working with a German landscape architect. The restaurant was to be sited by an artificial lake in the newly created Saffa Park in the centre of Dubai, in 1975 a city just emerging as a great moneyed mecca. When Gwynne arrived in the United Arab Emirates, however, he marched out of the meeting upon discovering that the developer had requested schemes by two other architects, returning only when he alone was promised the job. The scheme soon became even more complex when the ruler of Dubai wanted his own private banqueting house in the park, though that came to nothing. Gwynne also

THE ART OF LIVING 1960–84

In 1975, Gwynne's planned restaurant in Saffa Park, Dubai, was halted at the completion of the concrete shell and subsequently infilled by others as offices

found himself designing a set of concrete shells blossoming as the entrance gates to the park, as well as a fruit and vegetable market building. In the end, only the shell of the restaurant was constructed before work came to a halt and all communication broke down. Gwynne sued the businessman but the bailiffs got nothing back, although the man later ended up in prison for fraud.

The Dubai building, however, proved positive, to a point. The shell, like the M62 buildings, was a tent, or umbrella as Gwynne liked to call it, created by a circle of concrete ribs, perching like elegant spider legs that meet at a central peak (holding the water tank). It was to have been a first-class international restaurant, the interior with walls and ceilings cloaked in coloured mosaics, and enamel panels and tapestries by Knapp. Instead, the white exoskeleton was finished off inside by others, and today contains offices amidst the green open spaces of the park. With its eye-catching hexadecagon (16-sided) plan, Gwynne's pavilion building can be easily spotted in its green

85

setting from the heights of the city's many new skyscrapers, its geometric pattern anticipating the nearby artificial palm islands built 50 years later (see p. 146).

Forte had a weekend home not far from The Homewood, and would sometimes drop by to see Gwynne to discuss projects. His Ryde Farm Estate, near Ripley in Surrey, had 2,000 acres which he used for entertainment, including shoots. The house, a listed 17th-century timber-framed building, had a barn nearby, which Forte asked Gwynne in 1973 to convert, or it seems completely transform, as a more permanent base for his family. Gwynne designed a whole new house, comfortably appointed on a scale that the dining table had seating for 18 people (see p. 143). Even though the design stylistically had a touch of the traditional about it – the top floor of bedrooms was sequestered behind giant dormers – the local planning authority turned it down.

Forte's company also owned the Fairmile Hotel nearby, set back from the Portsmouth Road in a rural setting at Cobham. Originally a manor house, the hotel had gained a reputation for its food, and was attracting enough custom for Gwynne to be asked to add 30 bedrooms (see p. 146). Once again, he used a curve to advantage, setting the suites with their bedrooms and sitting rooms along an intersecting pair of semicircular corridors. But in 1978 the world's economy dipped into recession, while Forte found himself in a business power struggle, and the Fairmile Hotel scheme sank as a consequence.[8]

The largest project that thwarted Forte and Gwynne was a 100-bedroom addition to Malta's most famous hotel, the grand Hotel Phoenicia in Valetta, commissioned in 1966 when Forte purchased it. Building costs in Malta were cheap, and since the local currency was pegged to sterling, the island was proving attractive to British visitors and investors at a time when most foreign investment was restricted. The proposed site for the addition may have been historic, lying below the main hotel building, which nestles next to a section of the great fortifications of the Grand Knights, but Gwynne's design was thoroughly modern: a curvaceous J-shaped wing of bedrooms wrapping around a swimming pool with elevated views across the harbour (see p. 144). But when currency restrictions changed, Forte lost interest and moved on to more lucrative overseas hotel purchases.

But Malta still held good things for Gwynne. Within a year he was designing a smart apartment building in the north of the island. This was another collaboration with his friend, client and quantity surveyor Kenneth Monk, whom he had taken with him to advise on the Phoenicia project. Monk fell in love with Malta and purchased a fine building plot high on a hillside overlooking St Paul's Bay, the growing resort town named after the bay where St Paul was said to be shipwrecked on his way

THE ART OF LIVING 1960–84

Vista Point, St Paul's Bay, Malta, 1968, with staggered concrete balconies, stands high on a clifftop overlooking the Mediterranean

to Rome. When completed, Monk retained the top floor of the five-storey hi-rise as his winter getaway, the sale of the other flats financing the project. During the design stage, he purchased an adjacent site down the slope, so upon completion in 1968, Gwynne's upper block was linked by a garden, with a swimming pool, to a matching three-storey block below (*see* p. 145). All the luxurious apartments were split-level, making for principal elevations curiously broken in two. Externally, the large concrete balconies – The Homewood's 'drawers pulled out' type – were arranged in a staggered pattern to give, as Gwynne described it, 'the building a dramatic effect'. Monk's penthouse, the largest and most extravagant at twice the size of the other apartments, had an outside terrace as large as the great master bedroom, and no fewer than eight balconies in all four directions. Gwynne was obliged by law to take on a Maltese architect for the project. His partner was no less than Dom Mintoff, the country's anti-British Labour leader and sometime prime minister, whom Gwynne thought 'pleasant and polite'. Known as *Il-Perit* – The Architect – Mintoff had his powerful fingers in many of the island's building projects. He liked Gwynne's design, but the architectural appreciation was not mutual; looking at some of Mintoff's buildings, Gwynne dismissed them as 'wildly embarrassing'.

The Maltese apartment block was appropriately named Vista Point. Two years later, in 1970, Monk gave the same name to the summer residence Gwynne built for him and his family in Angmering-on-Sea, West Sussex. The house is a compact gem, a sophisticated getaway that looks like it has escaped from the French Riviera. Focusing on the sea view at the end of the long lawn, the living area is on the upper floor with its large windows and comfortably wide balcony. Walls are white, inside and out, but areas of the interior pop with coloured tiles: a burnt-orange kitchen, a bathroom in mustard yellow, another in deep midnight blue. The staircase was another addition to Gwynne's curvaceous beauties.

The shape of the Sussex Vista Point is like a fantastic hourglass thanks to Gwynne's arithmetical skill in setting out the brickwork to exact dimensions so that ten straight walls are joined to create an illusion of flowing lines (*see* p. 143). The experimental roof shape that he had used more than two decades earlier on Bilsby's first house evolves at Vista Point into an exaggerated wave, dipping low over the front entrance, rising to curl at the ridge then sweeping down and out over the living space on the seaward side. The double carport and single garage have a sinuous plan. In another instance of maximum design control, Gwynne set out the garden too, using mainly hardy shrubs and plants that weathered the sea salt.

Monk's early death in 1971 meant that he enjoyed his Vista Point holiday homes for just a few years. Fortunately, the Maltese block, although now swamped by poorly built neighbouring apartments, remains an elegant example from a lost period of jet-set Mediterranean lifestyle, while the English Vista Point has been blessed by a succession of sympathetic owners.

Garden front (looking towards the sea), Vista Point, Angmering-on-Sea, Sussex

Gwynne's architectural drawing of plans, sections and elevations for Vista Point, Angmering-on-Sea, Sussex, dated 1968

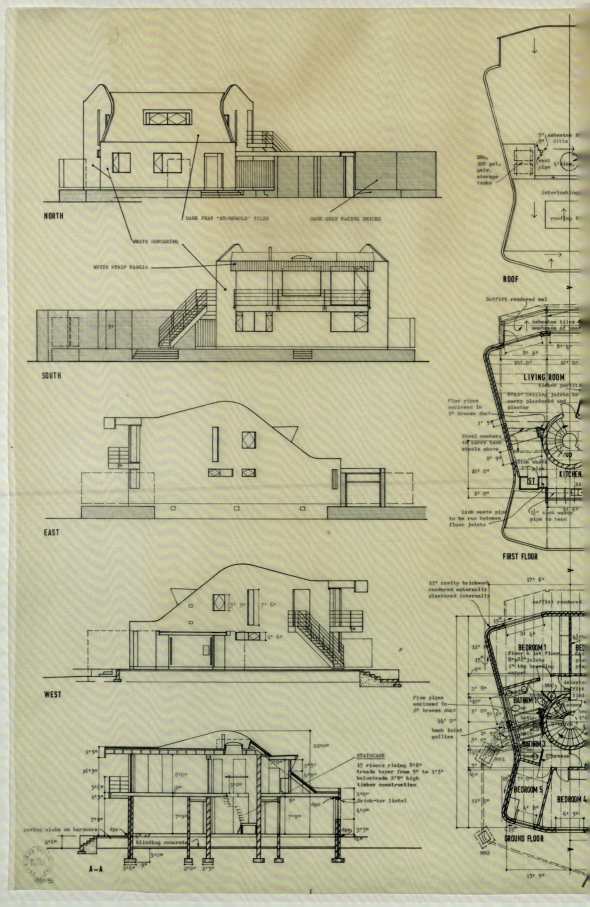

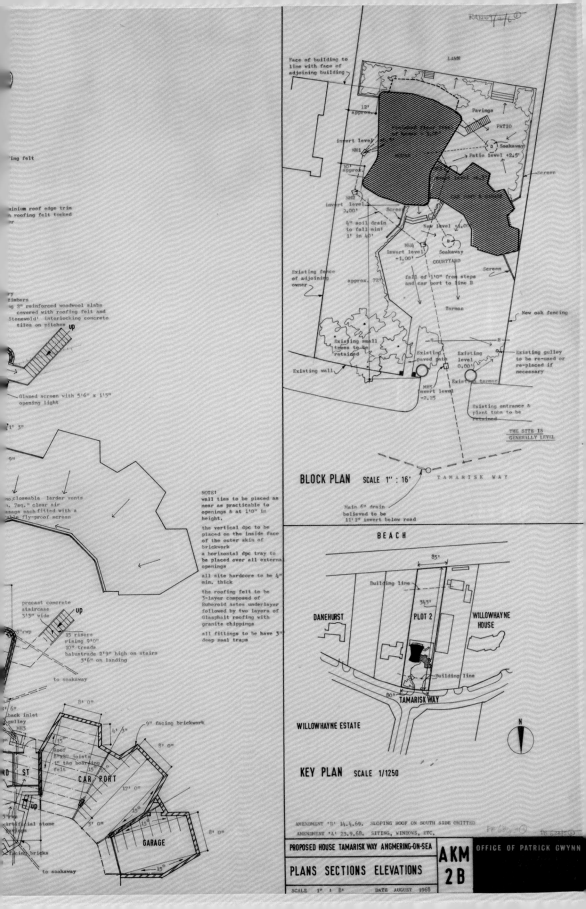

Internal stairs and living room, Vista Point, Angmering-on-Sea

No such luck followed Grovewood, the house Gwynne designed in 1965: it is now gone. On a woodland site on the Wentworth Estate, a rural enclave of country houses in Surrey, Gwynne had created a house in the shape of a Y, like a three-blade propeller when viewed from above, the same footprint as Connell's High and Over house of 1931 which had been such an early inspiration for Gwynne (see p. 142). The three wings housed the living room, bedrooms, kitchen and garage. The core of this two-storey house was a hexagon, with the six sides enclosing the entrance hall, staircase and dining room at ground level and, above, bathrooms and a dressing room. The great advantage of this unusual pattern was that it conformed to Gwynne's model of the separation of the three main functions of living, and stretched the house out so, like Witley Park, it afforded broad views in all directions, including to the garden where Gwynne added banks of ferns, heathers and rhododendrons.

Grovewood fell to what Gwynne considered 'greed'. After several decades of enjoying the house, the clients David and Jean Shaw sold up. The house went through another purchaser before the third owner demolished it around 1993, building an outsized neo-classical house in its place. Gwynne tried to be stoic about its disappearance, although such things stung: 'The only bonus point of buildings being pulled down is they then can't be made a mess of. I suppose the Shaw house, somebody might have done pretty nasty things to it, I prefer to see it gone forever myself.' It was another instance of Gwynne's way or no way.

In 1960, Leslie Bilsby asked Gwynne to design a new house for his family in Blackheath. Gwynne produced a novel yet practical design with a plan composed of three circles – the three main functions of domestic life (*see* p. 141). The larger space was for living and eating, the middle for bedrooms and the third for vehicles. To get the walls completely round, Gwynne proposed a steel frame with timber cladding. He presented the scheme to Bilsby by making a delightful architectural model with the three roofs rising by means of a toy motor to reveal the interior.[9] However, Gwynne was deluged with projects, having just completed the Hyde Park restaurants, working in Malta and about to embark on the York Theatre Royal extension. Bilsby therefore turned to the architect Walter Greaves, while replacing his 1949 Gwynne house with a large Span estate by Lyons.

Within a decade, ever itching for the novelty of a new house, in 1969 Bilsby once again turned to Gwynne. The result was 10 Blackheath Park, one of the most brazen modern houses of the period, its bronze-tinted glass and dark grey slate frontage to the street frequently stopping people in their tracks. In a leafy boulevard setting, bounded by imposing creamy Georgian houses, Bilsby's house is fortress-like, dark, slick and tough. The approach alone can be terrifying: the visitor is required to ascend a set of stairs, or the steep ramp originally intended for Bilsby's wheelchair-using mother, that twists around a pool and fountain, before crossing a metal bridge to the central front door, leaving the caller suspended several metres above the pavement below.

The façade of 10 Blackheath Park angles sharply because the plan is an X, a geometry more common to Renaissance star forts, like the one that dominates Valletta in Malta (*see* p. 142). Astonishingly, every corner room within is five-sided, a series of pentagons of equal diameter, joined by linking rooms and corridors clustered around an oval staircase. The continuous sequence of living spaces on the ground floor, a circular enfilade, was one that Bilsby wanted, especially for parties, because it could be divided off by pairs of pocket doors that were painted a vibrant glossy red. As with his other houses, Gwynne designed the furnishings to fit the mathematics: curving banquettes under the large windows, long steel and glass sideboards

Grovewood, West Drive, Wentworth Estate, Surrey, 1965 (demolished)

in the connecting spaces, and a useful centre island in the kitchen, five-sided, of course, to fit the room. Walls were covered in Gwynne's favourite Japanese grass paper (now more conveniently made in plastic imitation), and white fixtures set against contrasting dark brown and black tones, as in the master bathroom where the walls are panelled in black Vitrolite glass. The rear façade is nearly identical to the one facing the street, but with an

THE ART OF LIVING 1960–84

Gwynne made this model for a courtyard house (not built) for Leslie Bilsby, 1960

outdoor metal deck and a graceful staircase into the garden. Bilsby asked Ivor Cunningham, Lyons's partner who created many fine landscapes for Span, to lay out the garden. Down one side, Cunningham created a row of compartments edged with yew trees, each with a different feature, like a pond or roses.

Bilsby's wife Alexandra (Shura) died during the construction period, and with their two daughters now grown up, he married again, a friend whose husband had died about the same time. Annette Rigal was French, and while retaining 10 Blackheath Park, Bilsby moved with her to the Paris area, where he dabbled in French property development, commissioning Gwynne to design some speculative octagonally planned houses. But the marriage failed and, finding himself single again, Bilsby moved out of his Blackheath house and into a nearby Regency villa. He soon found a secluded and lengthy plot of land in the neighbourhood which had the little River Quaggy running through the bottom of the garden. Here Gwynne built him his third house.

Completed in 1979, 22 Parkgate was, said the architect, 'a real bachelor pad'. Gwynne first proposed a line of four angled and linked boxes, constructed in timber and clad in aluminium. But, as built, the structure revisited his 1960 design of three circles, now tweaked into three octagons

10 Blackheath Park, London, for Leslie Bilsby, 1969. The bronze-tinted glass and dark-grey slate front is approached over a metal bridge

and built in brick (*see* p. 143). A trio of eight-sided spaces were joined by rectangular link rooms. The copper-covered tent-like roofs were a scaled-down variant of the Dell Restaurant and Burtonwood buildings. The interior was tailored to Bilsby's request for studio living. At the centre of the largest octagon rose an impressive fireplace, around which seating, kitchen, dining and office areas were grouped within the single open space. One of the

Opposite top: View into living area, 10 Blackheath Park
Opposite: The garden room is between the living and dining rooms

THE ART OF LIVING 1960–84

smaller octagons was occupied by the master bedroom, and the other by the garage with small guest bedrooms above. The link rooms provided utilities like laundry and storage. The result was intimate yet spacious with high conical ceilings and long views down the garden.

Bilsby stayed in Parkgate until age and health required him to move in with one of his daughters. The new owners, Colin and Jacqui Hawkins, had two children, so to make the bachelor pad into a family home, Gwynne returned to convert the garage into a playroom and the service areas into the kitchen. As children's illustrators working from home, the Hawkinses had Gwynne convert the master bedroom into a studio space and add an additional storey overhead for their bedroom. Gwynne was very pleased with the conversion, although he refused to put a window on the new staircase between studio and master bedroom. The Hawkinses went ahead with the window anyway, and to their amusement – but not the architect's – on the day Gwynne climbed the stairs for the first time and noticed the window, he simply passed it in cool silence.

Bilsby always proved the perfect client, but not all of Gwynne's jobs ran so smoothly. Ananda House, expensive and rich in detail, was located on a twisting private road about a mile from The Homewood at 35 Meadway. It is gone now, demolished around the year 2000. The bitter battle over its construction exemplified Gwynne's exacting standards, or what others viewed as his persistent stubbornness.

The clients were Kenneth Knowles and his wife Muriel; drawings were being worked up from 1968. The design was another example of Gwynne's manipulation of brick, the shape being a very refined abstract that Gwynne called 'a waisted circle plan' (see p. 143). Bob King, Gwynne's young design assistant, did many of the working drawings. To capture the arc of a series of curves representing the walls, King recalled how he used a beam compass, one of an architect's biggest drawing instruments. Then the positioning of every brick was worked out exactly.[10] The garden front was especially attractive, a sculptural variation on the contemporary Vista Point, Angmering-on-Sea, with a sweeping first-floor balcony accessed by a spiral staircase. Inside, the living area had a fireplace set into a panoramic window. The curving brick walls and an undulating ceiling in Australian blackbean boarding improved the acoustic of the clients' music system and grand piano. Gwynne designed all the large built-in units and sourced soft furnishings like the sofa and chairs.

But the project hit a snag that other architects might have circumvented. The client asked that the planned hall corridor on the ground floor be wider by three inches. Gwynne would not budge. As Bob King said about Gwynne's attitude to his architecture, 'Patrick was basically saying: "Look, it's a total sculpture. You change one element and the whole fails."' Gwynne refused

THE ART OF LIVING 1960–84

22 Parkgate, Blackheath, London, 1979. Gwynne's third house for Leslie Bilsby, a cluster of three pavilions

the alteration and walked away from the job after seeing only the shell go up. He never saw the house again, even though it was just a few minutes from The Homewood. To complete Ananda, Knowles hired King, who had decided to move on after three years with Gwynne. The house was finished by 1971 much as Gwynne had designed it, but the Knowleses still pursued Gwynne for breach of contract. Nevertheless, Gwynne was willing when asked to contribute to an article for *Ideal Home*, which Knowles told the magazine editor that he found galling; the article never appeared.[11]

Also in 1971, Gwynne was working on a conversion and addition to an existing Edwardian house at 3 Kidderpore Avenue, Hampstead, for his most glitzy client, the actor Laurence Harvey. Born Zvi Mosheh Skikne in Lithuania in 1928, Harvey moved to England from South Africa when 18. Devilishly handsome, many people found him a charming social climber

99

The seating area around the central fireplace, 22 Parkgate, 1979

THE ART OF LIVING 1960–84

Living room of Ananda, looking towards the fireplace window, Esher, Surrey, 1971

not dissimilar to Joe Lampton, the character that gained him an Oscar nomination for best actor in *Room at the Top*, the 1959 British film with which he broke into Hollywood. He was an explosion of energy on and off stage and screen, damned by many actors in their autobiographies, yet adored by legions of fans and loyal Hollywood friends – and by Patrick Gwynne.

'Larry' loved to build. When young, he had begun to study architecture, so his success in films enabled him to indulge his mania for houses. In California, at his seafront Malibu place, Harvey often entertained his close friends like Elizabeth Taylor, Sammy Davis Jr and Peter Lawford. He commissioned three mansions from Conrad Buff and Donald Hensman, the society architects who in 1966 created the last Case Study House, No. 28, in a mid-century modern style that would have appealed greatly to Gwynne. Gwynne's introduction by Harvey to West Coast design culture had a strong influence on the Englishman's work, not only for Harvey's Hampstead commission but in the updates made at The Homewood.

Gwynne met Harvey in the late 1950s through his school friend Hugh Latimer, who had grown into a noted actor. The pair instantly hit it off – 'we got on like that', said Gwynne snapping his fingers.[12] 'He was', Gwynne would recall, 'one of the most engaging persons I ever met ... I suited him', and by 1959 Gwynne was meeting him on set. Harvey's private life was as tempestuous as that of any movie star. He appeared in juicy Hollywood tales, and his sister-in-law, who wrote the most authoritative (if flawed) biography on him, cited many examples of his bisexuality.[13]

From their very first meeting, Gwynne and Harvey talked about houses. Their initial venture was in 1961 when Gwynne designed a large country house for Harvey on a beautiful hilltop site in Windlesham, Surrey, on Westwood Road (see p. 142). But just as the machinery came in to dig the foundations, claimed Gwynne, the whole thing was scuppered when Harvey moved to America. It was not until 1971 that Harvey and Gwynne had the chance to work together on the Hampstead house. By then, Harvey was separated from his second wife and was now with the much younger Paulene Stone, a major British fashion model of the Swinging Sixties, a *Vogue* cover girl photographed by Patrick Lichfield, John French and David Bailey. Larry and Paulene appeared together, newly married, on the July 1972 cover of *Cosmopolitan*. As Harvey was a resident of California and thus not legally domiciled in Britain, the house was in Paulene's name. The couple now had two children, Sophie by Stone's first marriage, who would become an architect – Gwynne proudly presenting her with a full set of Le Corbusier's *Oeuvre Complète* upon her graduation from Yale University – and Domino, who grew up to be a bounty hunter and was semi-fictionally portrayed by the actress Kiera Knightley in the 2005 action crime film *Domino*.

As the Hampstead house was, as Gwynne called it, 'quite dreadful', Harvey suggested that Paulene and Gwynne, who had not met yet, join him in Italy on location in order to discuss plans for its rebuilding. So Gwynne picked her up in his Aston Martin and they drove over, putting the car on a plane at Lympne to cross the Channel. Paulene found Gwynne 'terrific ... a gentleman' and they 'never stopped talking the whole time down'; she especially enjoyed his love of food.[14] They became good friends for life.

Gwynne gutted the house they had bought and with Harvey's decorative flair turned it into a movie star's mansion (see p. 143). The exterior was stripped of its bays, the surfaces flattened in vertical white-rendered panels with tinted windows in black frames. On the garden there was a new sunroom, with a studio added to the side, decked out with a bar, a sofa designed by Gwynne, and a pair of Eames lounge chairs and ottomans, one of which became Gwynne's favourite chair when Paulene gave it to him. The studio, strictly for Harvey's sole use, had its own entrance and was over the garage, sauna, jacuzzi and changing facilities for the new swimming pool. For Harvey, a devotee of the barbecue, Gwynne created a patio grill station with a fixed dining table in his distinctive boomerang shape facing the action; the surrounding walls were hung with sculpture and one of Knapp's enamels.

THE ART OF LIVING 1960–84

Gwynne's clients and friends, the newly married actor Lawrence Harvey and supermodel Paulene Stone, by fashion photographer Brian Duffy. A similar photograph from the photo shoot appeared on the front cover of British *Cosmopolitan* magazine, July 1972

Inside the house, Gwynne rejigged the layout of the rooms, put in false ceilings and added tiled kitchen and bathrooms. For casual seating, there was the new pavilion on the garden side. Harvey had a sideline in antiques, with a shop in Los Angeles (by Buff and Hensman), and all his homes were chocked with extravagant pieces, not to Gwynne's taste at all, but in Hampstead the heavy stuffed furniture and walls covered in gilt rococo mirrors made for comfortable opulence.

Larry and Paulene moved into 3 Kidderpore Avenue over Easter 1971. Gwynne was a frequent guest, photographed enjoying lively times with the family in the garden or partying with stars like Michael Caine and Joan

Laurence Harvey's study, 3 Kidderpore Avenue, Hampstead, London, 1971

The grill station and dining table with director's chairs on the patio of the Laurence and Paulene Harvey house, 1971

Collins. Gwynne had joined the Harveys and their crowd on the French Riviera in 1970, including a New Year's Eve dinner in St Tropez and visits to Ventimiglia. Larry and Paulene looked glamorous in full-length fur coats, with the group driven around in Harvey's Rolls Royce by his white-gloved uniformed chauffeur. The group called in at St Paul-de-Vence to see Leslie Bricusse, the Academy Award-winning English composer of film music like *Goldfinger*. This meeting led to another of Harvey's unfulfilled capers, with Gwynne coming up with an idiosyncratic design for a pair of identical houses set in the rocky hillside of St Paul, one for Harvey, the other for Bricusse, great concrete tents, ten-sided and luxuriously appointed (*see* p. 143). Paulene also took Gwynne with her in 1972 to California as a surprise for Harvey. They stayed at the Malibu house and partied with Zsa Zsa Gabor. Harvey had found a vacant lot nearby and Gwynne drew up a design for a new beach house, with a separate guest wing, but like Harvey's other architectural dreams, this came to nothing (*see* p. 143).

The idyll ended too soon when, in November 1973, Harvey died of cancer aged only 45. In her autobiography, Paulene wrote poignantly of Harvey on his deathbed (a great Tudoresque four poster) in Kidderpore Avenue with a hysterical Elizabeth Taylor rushing in and acting the drama queen.[15] Paulene and the girls stayed on in the house until Easter 1975, when she sold it; in subsequent years it was much altered.

After Ananda House and his work for Harvey, building commissions slowed for Gwynne. It was a sign of the times. The oil crisis of 1973 sparked a recession and the building world, including Gwynne, felt the downturn. He was unsuccessful that year in a competition for new Parliamentary Offices in Bridge Street, across from the Houses of Parliament. He dabbled with house designs for people he knew, including the director of a brick company who had a site in Abinger Common, Surrey, and drew up plans for a restaurant and pub in Ampney Crucis, Gloucestershire, again with no outcome.

Gwynne then found a client who, far from suffering economically, was an American oil and timber magnate, said to be the world's wealthiest private individual, riding high on the 1970s oil crisis. He met Stanley J Seeger in 1979 through his nephew George Cruddas, who had just begun working as the tycoon's personal assistant. Seeger had recently fallen in love with Christopher Cone and swept him off to Greece; they became life partners. Returning to England, Seeger began to acquire a series of properties, including one of Britain's most famous Tudor country houses, Sutton Place in Surrey. Cruddas, trained as an architect, became project manager for the estate and Gwynne, although but one of Seeger's several architects, undertook a number of projects for the new couple.

With his quiet gentlemanly nature, and no doubt his unspoken homosexuality, Gwynne felt at home in Seeger's exceedingly shy and very private world. Like Harvey, Seeger loved collecting and selling artworks, antique and modern, but with a connoisseur's eye and on a scale that was legendary; his sale of 88 Pablo Picasso paintings in 1993 made headline news. Sutton Place overflowed with his acquisitions; guests famously found themselves greeted in the great hall with the grotesque writhing figures of naked men in a large Francis Bacon triptych. Seeger commissioned the landscape architect Geoffrey Jellicoe to create one of Britain's most famous 20th-century gardens. Gwynne's addition of a new squash court was more modest. Attached to the existing tennis court, this small structure, faced in vertical tongue-and-groove boarding, housed the playing court with a viewing platform and changing facilities. So discreet was Gwynne and Seeger's professional relationship that no official photographs were taken of any of their projects.

When Gwynne was introduced to Seeger and Cone, they were living in Hays Mews, Mayfair, and his first job was to add a sauna. The couple also owned a Georgian house nearby, 49 Berkeley Square, where Cruddas was co-ordinating three architects in its transformation and asked 'Uncle Pat' to design the top-floor flat. However, the couple did not stay long and in 1981 Gwynne created a spectacular new flat for them at 26 St James's Place, the modern apartment building overlooking Green Park designed in 1958–9 by Denys Lasdun. Occupying a whole floor, the apartment was encased in panoramic windows. Gwynne gutted the interior and fashioned a sleek, rich replacement: the doors of the wall fitments and wardrobes were faced in glass, the small staircase to the sunken reception area had marble treads, the kitchen a marble floor and an automatic sliding door. And there was a sauna. The overall tone was warm, with chocolate-coloured walls. It was all state of the art, Gwynne at his luxurious best. But Seeger, ever a restless character, stayed only six years at Sutton Place. And after he and Cone moved from St James's Place, Gwynne's work was removed.

In 1984, Gwynne built his last house. Winterdown was another job with problems between himself and his client, Robin Fawcett, a dealer in cultured pearls, and wife Georgina, a physician. They had purchased a secluded gamekeeper's cottage, to be replaced by Gwynne's new house, set in extensive grounds deep in Winterdown Woods on the hill immediately southwest of The Homewood; the two Gwynne houses are visible in the distance to one another when the trees are bare of leaves. The geometry of Gwynne's plan was simpler than in many of his houses, like a butterfly with swept-back wings. Gwynne called it a 'part-moon plan'. Mustard-yellow brick was used on the exterior of the ground floor and the sinuous walls surrounding the garage and swimming pool, as well as inside – save in the bedrooms, which were plastered. Gwynne treated the first floor with a streamlined modern mansard roof which was inset with windows and doors, some with balconies. Forming the heart of the plan was the large central

THE ART OF LIVING 1960–84

Winterdown, Portsmouth Road, Esher, Surrey, 1984

entrance hall, with one of Gwynne's fine open staircases in hardwood, the garden side overlooking an ornamental pond. One of the wings contains the living space, with a large log fireplace, and the adjoining kitchen, which became the point of contention. Fawcett, an aficionado of Japanese cuisine, did all the cooking in the house and arranged for Gwynne to create a large kitchen island with a great grilling plate and plenty of space to sit around. Gwynne was disappointed that the joiners did such a poor job on the unit, but before he had time to make changes the client removed it and had a shop-bought replacement installed. Gwynne announced: 'So, I said, I won't visit the house again'. And he never did, although Georgina remained a friend, often visiting him at The Homewood.

Another project of note in the 1980s was Gwynne's entry in one of the country's most famous and shameful architectural competitions: the extension to the National Gallery on the northwest corner of Trafalgar Square, the same site for which he entered the 1958–9 contest. In 1982, Gwynne was one of 79 entrants. Unsurprisingly, his plan was geometric, comprising a bundle of irregular octagons with two longer sides that would have presented rows of tall pods to the square. He was fortunate not to have become involved in the ensuing controversy.

After Winterdown, Gwynne took on a few small jobs. In 1986, Bilsby had him design a row of shops and offices on a site opposite Blackheath Station. Faced in brick and with a mansard roof, its plan was unusual: a U-shaped arrangement of five rectangles each chamfered at the corners.[16] But the local

107

National Gallery extension, Trafalgar Square, competition entry model, 1982

amenity society was not keen to see the Victorian arcade of shops disappear and the scheme was dropped. Another unsuccessful scheme the same year was for a block of four apartments near Monk's house in Tamarisk Way, Angmering-on-Sea, Sussex. Arranged so that all the living rooms overlooked the Channel, each of the four outer corners of the building were marked by fully glazed bay windows from ground to eaves.[17]

In a small but satisfying job, Gwynne helped Vivien Griffiths to alter a 1938–9 house at 2 South Parade, Bedford Park, designed by émigré architect Fritz (Frederick) Ruhemann working with Michael Dugdale, briefly of Tecton. It had been recorded by Dell & Wainwright, who had photographed The Homewood the previous year, and published in the *Architectural Review* for February 1939. The original Austrian clients lived entirely in a large room on the raised ground floor, with an elaborate fold-out bed. Griffiths' applications to alter the sunroom on the flat roof into a master bedroom of a listed building were turned down by the local planning authority and English Heritage. The story even reached Piloti's column in *Private Eye*, which strongly disapproved of Griffiths' plans. In December 1994, she opened a *Sunday Times* colour supplement and discovered an article about The Homewood.

She approached Gwynne, who quickly created a design that met with official approval. At the suggestion of conservationists, he added a delicate pergola on the roof reminiscent of that already existing there.

Completed in 1999, Gwynne's addition was minimal, set back, and in terms of conservation, in keeping. Echoing the 1930s original, he installed a glass-brick patio screen at the entrance to the house, which bore an uncanny resemblance to that at The Homewood, giving privacy from the neighbours, and extending to join effortlessly to the Art Deco sweep of the original canopy. The interior, designed to Griffiths' requests, was a bedroom open to the sky, with a series of four rooflights. Gwynne pulled out his technical wizardry with motorised blinds overhead and a bespoke cabinet at the bottom of the bed for the television to rise and fall electrically.[18]

The following year, Gwynne produced drawings for converting the garage area at 2 South Parade into a guest suite. His health, however, was failing and he was not fit enough to travel into London to oversee the building work. Griffiths visited him regularly for instructions and, using her contacts in the building trade, even helped him source furnishings for The Homewood. Very fond of him, she recalled that 'he was a manipulative old thing but I was happy to do his bidding in the end'.[19] Gwynne only saw the completed Bedford Park suite in photographs. He was now 87 years old, yet in the midst of one of his most intensely productive periods.

6   The Homewood 1940–2003

After the war, Patrick Gwynne and his sister Babs returned to The Homewood, the house now jointly theirs. The house made its public reappearance soon after, in June 1946 on the cover of the popular *Ideal Home* magazine.[1]

Many friends drifted through for short stays during these early years while looking for permanent accommodation. Babs moved on, marrying William Cruddas in December 1945; the couple occupied one of the cottages in the garden until finding a house in Essex. Babs sold her half of the house and property to Patrick, who had to release substantial assets to recompense her. Brother and sister, who always got on well, found the arrangement convenient.

Gwynne lived in the house until his death in 2003. Over those near six decades, he made many changes, none drastic, all enriching. The Homewood of 1938 always shone through these later alterations and additions, which were mainly a flourish of interior furnishings of his own design and replacements of worn-out fixtures and fittings. He also gradually transformed the ten acres of grounds into a 'woodland garden', as he preferred to call it, 'not a park'.

As his architectural commissions gradually increased after the war, Gwynne worked from home, moving into his father's study on the ground floor, close to the front door for callers.[2] In the 1960s, he refitted the space with furniture and fittings to his own design, beautifully detailed and executed. There was a circular table with a terrazzo pedestal for meetings, a fixed side table and chair of white tubular steel for conversation, along with a fine selection of classic modern chairs by Eero Saarinen, Arne Jacobsen and Harry Bertoia. Gwynne's long desk, of his own design, poised on a great terrazzo pedestal, accommodated a drawing board, a work and writing surface and integrated telephone switchboard, a command station worthy of the bridge of the Starship *Enterprise* in the new TV series *Star Trek*. Behind was a wall-to-wall cabinet with more work surface and a sleek geometry of drawers, one with a touch-to-open mechanism releasing an electric

Gwynne added the large enamelled steel panels by the artist Stefan Knapp to The Homewood in the 1960s

Patrick Gwynne in his studio office, The Homewood, 1992

typewriter – Gwynne preferred typing his correspondence, both office and personal, neatly on headed letter paper. The use of each drawer was precisely worked out for drawing instruments, paper and materials. In the detail, Gwynne found the pleasure of an organised life.

When commissions came in a quick succession in 1960 and staff were needed, he converted his parents' bedroom suite on the first floor of the house into a drawing studio, well away from his office but connected by his exchange. He first engaged John Grey as his assistant, succeeded by Robert (Bob) King, in 1966 fresh out of the Northern Polytechnic.[3] King was soon joined by two technicians, Richard Patten and Tony Miller, who were responsible for the detailed technical drawings and for supervising York Theatre Royal on site; they were, said King, 'the guys who knew how to screw it together'.[4] Later, in the mid-1970s, when his staff had departed, Gwynne took on for the summer months a couple of architecture students, his nephew George Cruddas and Oliver Richards (later of ORMS). Gwynne also had several secretaries, of whom Elvine Cottrell was the longest serving, from 1963 to 1971. She sat in the entrance hall at the foot of the stairs at a small desk that Gwynne designed for her and which she had to roll away into a cubbyhole at the end of the day.[5]

Gwynne was a demanding boss, and at times 'not easy to work with', remembered Cottrell; he could be 'nippy'.[6] But he was also generous, giving her lovely Christmas presents every year. And when King announced his engagement, Gwynne took him and his fiancée to a very smart restaurant and raised his salary. Gwynne did not, however, tolerate insubordination. Leaving the office was almost an act of disloyalty; being from a military family, Gwynne expected that staff would serve under him unquestioningly. When King chose to go after three years to finish Ananda house, Gwynne was 'very angry'; they 'fell out' and never spoke again. King was generous about the snub, saying that he saw it 'in a way a compliment'. When Miss Cottrell (Gwynne never once called her by her first name, nor she by his) got a job in Libya, he handed her a beautiful bag as a leaving gift on her last day, saying with a touch of dry irony, 'You don't deserve it', and without a goodbye turned and walked away.[7] In later years, when asked the names of his architectural staff, he sometimes said, 'I forget'.

Gwynne's drawing method and style derived from his early training. In Wells Coates's office he had absorbed the engineered look beloved of modernists, mainly using black ink with much use of the straightedge to precisely capture the new rectangularity of the architecture. The drawings may have looked contemporary, but they still relied upon centuries-old architectural drawing skills using ruling pens, the ink brushed into the gap between two metal points which were adjusted to the width of the desired line. In the late 1950s, always the lover of new gadgets, Gwynne purchased the easy-to-use Rapidograph pen by Rotring, with its changeable nib sizes for line width, using the 0.3mm line generally, the 0.5mm for details like complicated brickwork, and 0.8 for lettering. He also had a typewriter with an oversized carriage for lettering on large drawing paper to reinforce the mechanised impression of the design. And he was quick to use new products when they came onto the market, such as self-adhesive labels and plastic stretched polyester drawing sheets like Mylar. For duplicating drawings, Gwynne owned a dyeline print machine, a luxury in a small office like his, but a necessity as The Homewood was far from copy shops.

To draw the buildings based on his signature curving line, Gwynne used one of the most ancient of draughting tools, the compass; and for large circles and curves with extended radii, out came his metal beam-compass, several feet long. Irregular swoops required a set of wooden French curves, and when they came into production, he bought the plastic ones. The use and skill with these architectural drawing instruments formed the basis of Gwynne's drawn architecture, translating into the highly unusual geometric forms in his built work.

Gwynne sometimes illustrated his projects with finished perspectives, although in later years these tended to be more freehand sketches, made during briefs to his clients, rendered in coloured pencil or his favourite felt-tip pen. The fluidity of being able to throw off ideas by sketching with a great deal of accuracy impressed clients. 'He drew beautifully', said his client Dr Salmon: 'He'd draw a dead-straight line, 45 degrees or 70 degrees, just like that'.[8] Gwynne and his team would on occasion make models, most notably for the Serpentine Restaurant. All these models have disappeared, with the exception of that crafted for the unbuilt 1960 Courtyard House for Leslie Bilsby.[9]

Besides his architectural staff, Gwynne also had a live-in housekeeper. Mrs Lily Wright and her husband, Bert, who worked in London, resided in the small but comfortable flat that Gwynne had formed in the servants' wing, upgrading it to suit the couple. Conscientious, and an excellent seamstress, Mrs Wright ran the house to Gwynne's exacting standards.[10] Ted Baldwin was Gwynne's gardener for 25 years from the 1950s to 1970s before his relatively early death. He was widowed and lived in the Garden Cottage in the grounds with his children who were mostly away at school. Deferential, he always began his requests with 'Mr Gwynne, sir.'[11] Baldwin managed the apple orchard, raised asparagus and lettuce that was collected by a van from Harrods, and planted out a large plot of blue spruce for sale as Christmas trees. Gwynne also sent him out to plant the gardens of several of his new houses.

Although Gwynne was a man happy in his own company, Geoffrey Rand lived with him at The Homewood for about ten years from the late 1950s.[12] Rand had a boyfriend for at least part of the time.[13] An accomplished pianist, he composed small pieces and arrangements, several of which were published, very contemporary works like *Perpetual Motion* (1961), a four-part song for unaccompanied voices. He had worked for the popular daily BBC radio programme *Children's Hour* alongside Violet Carson, an excellent pianist who later became famous as an actress as the character Ena Sharples in *Coronation Street*.[14] Gwynne purchased a new Bechstein boudoir grand piano for him, replacing his mother's, and designed two cabinets for sheet music. Rand was highly strung and nervous, and Gwynne tended to be the dominant character. They led relatively separate lives, with adjoining bedrooms and single beds, although they did many things together, like attending the opening of the Serpentine Restaurant. Visiting America as a member of the Unitarian Church, Rand became ill. He returned to The Homewood for a short time, but appears to have suffered a stroke and died soon after at the age of 42. Gwynne always kept a photograph of him on the sideboard in the living room, a handsome young man in evening dress seen at the piano, leaning into the keyboard during a recital.

One friendship which had a lasting effect on Gwynne's life began in 1963 when he met the 19-year-old Raymond Menzies who one day appeared, curious about the house, having seen it many times when out

The pianist and composer Geoffrey Rand lived with Gwynne for more than a decade from the late 1950s

fishing in the local streams. They struck up a lifelong friendship and working relationship. Raymond and his wife Janet became indispensable in Gwynne's life and significant in The Homewood's survival; with their children Tyanne, Tina and Stefan they became like family to Gwynne. After the live-in staff departed, Janet helped clean the house on weekends as a favour. She and Gwynne found food their common passion; she came from a farming family and was an excellent cook. Gwynne, ever the epicurean, would plan elaborate meals with Janet, especially for their Christmases together.

Gwynne enjoyed entertaining. He was quick-witted with a dry sense of humour, always making quips, rarely sarcastic and with a self-deprecating manner, one that could easily deflect any sensitive questioning, like matters about his private life. He would throw parties at The Homewood once or twice a year, sometimes for up to 70 people. Miss Cottrell recalled one typical party about 1970 when she and the other staff spent hours preparing fresh strawberries, lobster and champagne for a gathering that included Laurence Harvey and Paulene Stone, Jack Hawkins, Denys Lasdun and Bernard Jay, a young friend whom Gwynne had met working at the Theatre Royal, York, and who stayed at The Homewood for a short time while finding

Raymond Menzies by the newly dugout ponds at The Homewood, 1971. Menzies and his wife Janet helped Gwynne with the house and garden for forty years

a new position.[15] The staff, of course, were relegated to pushing food and drink through the hatch.

As his income from commissions increased between the 1950s and the 1970s, Gwynne began a gradual process of revitalising and improving The Homewood. There was a continuous necessary upgrading, for example with the inadequate heating and failing window frames. But in the 1980s and 1990s Gwynne's finances dwindled and his principal source of income was the rent of the cottages on his property, which also had to be maintained.

One of his first jobs at The Homewood in the post-war years was to renovate the kitchen to a high standard. With his ever-increasing interest in cooking and cuisine, specialist knowledge in catering from working for Lord Forte and creating speciality kitchens in many private houses, Gwynne felt he needed a new 'fairly professional kitchen, not one that you sit around and watch the television in'.[16] The first of many makeovers was the boldest, eradicating the partition walls that created separate areas for the cook and maids to make a single space, although he kept a low tiled partition to divide the cooking section from a small working area. Progressively, he upgraded the kitchen with features of his own design, including a great overhead uplighter with ceiling rails for hanging copper pans, the contraption dangling over one of his signature island counters that he had personally tiled in chocolate brown to match the walls and cupboards. Ever the stylist, when *Country Life* magazine came to photograph the kitchen in 1993, Gwynne arranged the setting as he had done many times over the decades for photo shoots of his interiors, this time placing vegetables on a trolley of his own design like a Dutch still life and posing crockery, eggs and flour on the centre island as if caught in the midst of baking.[17]

Besides changing his parents' suite into a staff office, Gwynne reduced the three central bedrooms into two, giving himself and Rand larger rooms. He replaced the rusted steel frame windows in the bedrooms with softwood frames. To the existing built-in furniture, he added upholstered bedframes with concealed lighting. It was a fine upgrade, but that monkish aesthetic remained, a quality of its architect.

The living and dining spaces retained their 1930s framework but were rearranged and refurnished; with the majority of pieces designed by Gwynne, a bespoke princely layer of mid-century modern was added to the history of the house. A home cinema enthusiast, he created a heavy couch concealing a projection screen that cranked up from behind its back. Its companion piece was an elegant long table, placed in front of the great window overlooking the garden, its pigskin top hiding a small compartment made for holding a cinefilm splicer; Gwynne possessed an excellent German film projector to show his home movies. The French walnut veneer of the wall of cabinetry faded over time from the light of the windows opposite and was replaced by Indian laurel. The great panoramic window was fitted twice with electrically operated Venetian blinds that gracefully rose up and down in a slow performance.

The dining room retained its beautiful display wall and serving hatch.[18] The original rectangular table, however, was replaced by one of Gwynne's magical futuristic designs: upon a pedestal base composed of two spun aluminium cones, the large circular table top is of grey-tinted glass sprayed black on the reverse, the edge in plated steel; a central well holds a Perspex flower bowl lit by a trio of coloured lights that were controlled by a set of knobs at the host's fingertips. Across the room from his dining chair hung the four Regency ancestral portraits in slim new metal frames, from where, Gwynne joked, 'they sit looking out on what they probably don't approve of'.

Gwynne structurally left the original exteriors of The Homewood unchanged. He did, however, have problems with the wall surfaces: his father's Stic B failed, and a series of masonry paints including Glamorock in the 1960s, Sandtex, and then the liquid plastic Decadex all caused difficulties. He added a fountain to the oval pool that Denys Lasdun had designed when the house was built. And it was Lasdun who introduced Gwynne to the artist Stefan Knapp, who created the dozen large enamelled steel panels that are now so much a feature of the garden façade. Made to fit the module

Gwynne designed a desk for the living room that could be transformed into a drawing board

The fireplace corner of the living room of The Homewood

THE HOMEWOOD 1940–2003

The built-in wall unit in the living room with a serving table that swings out

unit of the house, the abstract panels are flowing swirls of rich blues, blacks and hints of copper that create the effect of sky and water reflecting off the building.[19]

Influenced by his time with Harvey, Gwynne added touches of Californian lifestyle. In 1974, he designed a swimming pool with a plan as uniquely shaped as one of his houses, and converted part of the servants' quarters into a sauna, with built-in speakers, a sunlamp and changing area. Beneath the patio overhang, the space originally created for a ping-pong table was turned into a sophisticated dining area. The outdoor fireplace and chimney were converted to an American gas barbecue and surrounded by fitted counters with a hot plate, warming cupboard, sink, dishwasher and crockery storage. Guests sat at the counter on high stools, listening to music from the outdoor speakers while feasting on one of Gwynne's gourmet grills. For 1970s

The dining room

England, home outdoor entertainment in such intimate fine-dining style was extremely novel.

The garden became a great focus for Gwynne as he improved on what his father had begun. Foremost was the removal of a stand of oaks close to the house, thereby opening up a sweeping view the near length of the property, improved by the replacement of the large market garden and orchard with lawns and woodland, although Gwynne and Menzies retained a sizable kitchen garden for their own use. A major new feature was the damming of the stream to create a series of ponds that Gwynne considered important for the reflection of the sky when seen from the house. Again, his friend Menzies volunteered for the big mechanical digging and labour. A highlight of the garden had been the maples introduced by his father in the 1930s; these he greatly supplemented, making for a colourful autumn spectacle. Then, like adding rooms to a house, Gwynne designed a sequence of specialist gardens: one for grasses, another a thicket of bamboo and ferns, the 'blue and white garden', the 'grey and yellow garden', the heather patch, the variegated and fern walk and the bog garden.

As Gwynne grew older he began to consider the future of The Homewood. It had been listed for its special architectural interest in 1971, which covered the exterior and bones of the interior, but not its contents. He felt his nieces and nephews were comfortably settled and would not wish to take on the burden. Pivotally, in 1992, Gwynne was introduced to Lady Pat Gibberd, the widow of the architect Sir Frederick Gibberd, who was struggling to preserve the house and garden that she and her husband had created in Harlow, Essex.[20] Sitting with Gwynne on his terrace, she suggested future options, among them the National Trust. This prompted Gwynne to contact his old friend, Michael Manser, a Trust advisor. The ball started rolling. Manser rallied the Trust's executive and team to consider the house as a gift. In the early 1990s, the appreciation and preservation of inter-war architecture was on the rise, and although the Trust had no examples of Modern Movement houses in its portfolio, it was then considering Ernö Goldfinger's house of 1939 in Hampstead. These were, in fact, the only two examples of major pre-1939 modernist houses in England to have survived with original contents. But some advisors did not regard The Homewood as 'outstanding', a major clause of the Trust's mandate, especially because it was not a pure example of the period, its 1960s and 1970s overlay deeply unfashionable for many by the 1990s.[21]

Another problem, however, was that in order to accept it, the Trust needed an endowment for the property to be maintained in perpetuity. Income from visitors would not be enough, so the idea of paying tenants proved perfect for the Trust and for Gwynne who never saw The Homewood as a personal shrine but always as a family home. He was very insistent that it should be let, and only to a family.

A campaign began to raise the profile of the house and articles on Gwynne and the house appeared in style magazines and national newspapers during 1993 and 1994. The Trust accepted it in 1994. Less than a year later, in January 1995, The Homewood starred in the opening sequence of the television documentary *Treasures in Trust* shown on the BBC. Lounging in his Eames chair, Gwynne explained his decision: 'I have no offspring or relatives [Babs had died in 1989] who would want, who would be able to live in the house. And I thought that if it was put on the market after my time it would certainly be bought by the wrong people'. Gwynne had seen too many of his own buildings disappear or gutted.[22]

In the agreement, the Trust restored the house and garden while he continued to live there. For almost a decade, Gwynne and the National Trust cohabited, not always comfortably. Gwynne had his views and the Trust had its, and a budget. Problematically, Gwynne was not in the least concerned with historic conservation; as an early modern architect, he had only the most general appreciation for the past. As he wrote to the Trust, 'I have never and do not look upon the house as a "period piece".[23] His view of The Homewood's future was somewhat influenced by the example of his nephew George Cruddas, who with his partner Christopher Dunkley tenanted a large

Patrick Gwynne and Lady Gibberd on the terrace of The Homewood discussing the future of the house, 1992

grade I-listed early 18th-century house in Somerset owned by the Trust. The difference, however, was that their property was let unfurnished and not regularly open to the public, whereas The Homewood was, in all but name, an inhabited museum. Gwynne's approach to what could stay, be renewed or simply thrown away was personal and at times cavalier. Worn pieces of his own design – furniture, wall fitments, whole room settings – could go. 'If things get worn out, then they can be replaced', he said casually.[24] Fortunately, this view was not adopted by the Trust.

However, Gwynne could not be persuaded all of the time. On a few occasions, his steely resolve won over opposition, most notably in his insistence on 'returning' the main bedroom suite. For more than half the life of the house, his parents' suite had been fitted out as the staff office. This was a key room in its history, with its plan chests, drawing boards and dyeline printing machine – a rare survivor of a modern architect's office and integral to understanding how the house was used. Nevertheless, the office was stripped and the room made into a bedroom.

With great good fortune, he and the appointed architects hit it off. John Allan and Fiona Lamb of Avanti Architects had a long and respected track record in the restoration of modern buildings in Britain, and would go on to work sensitively on other Gwynne houses with the master's blessing. Because Gwynne held Allan and Lamb in high regard, they were able to keep his unhistorical views within boundaries. Nevertheless, dozens of well-meaning Trust advisors and workers became the target of his stinging letters and silent moods. Nightly, when everyone had gone home, he would inspect the day's work and in the morning there was a good chance that the site agent would find yesterday's job covered in reproachful sticky notes.[25]

Allan found Gwynne 'patrician' and 'an old sage', and together they treated The Homewood like a puzzle box to be put together better than ever.[26] The flat roof needed extensive work, and there was general electrical rewiring (Allan persuaded Gwynne to retain the 1930s rocker switches although they did not meet modern standards) along with a thousand and one other repairs. Avanti received hundreds of faxes, drawings and comments spiced with Gwynne's dry humour. There were many conversations over interior colours, and in the end no fewer than seven shades of grey were used throughout the house. The work took over a year, with the house in scaffolding and Gwynne living in the staff quarters which had been done up first.

The project gave Gwynne, now in his eighties, renewed vigour. He prepared extensive reports, hundreds of pages long: inventories of the furniture, information on construction and services, and a detailed ring binder on the garden, illustrated with drawings showing it as is and what he envisioned, his holy scripture for the Trust to try and abide by.[27] There was even a full page on the 'rabbit menace' (best solution: clearing the undergrowth and shooting them).

With work completed, Gwynne moved back into the main part of the house. He became increasingly frail, not helped by seriously injuring himself falling off a ladder. He was slightly deaf, and had received a pacemaker and a hip replacement. He was watched over by the Menzies who were now living in the Garden Cottage. Raymond continued doing many jobs and errands, although the Trust increasingly took on roles like maintaining the garden. Every morning before going to work, Janet collected cheerful notes left out by Gwynne of his latest news and precise shopping requests often illustrated by helpful little drawings of the desired items.

Patrick Gwynne died in a cot by his bedroom window at The Homewood on 3 May 2003, in his 90th year. The evening before, he had requested that his ashes be buried under a tree in the garden with, naturally, a party. His wish was fulfilled: friends and relatives gathered for a last celebration in his beloved house before accompanying him to his resting place in his glorious woodland garden.

Notes

Foreword
1. John Potvin, *Bachelors of a Different Sort: Queer Aesthetics, Material Culture and the Modern Interior in Britain* (Manchester: Manchester University Press, 2014), p. 24.
2. Le Corbusier, *Almanach de l'Architecture Moderne* (Paris: Crès, 1926), p. 29.

Preface
1. *The Times*, 8 May 2003, p. 39; *The Guardian*, 8 May 2003, p. 31; *The Daily Telegraph*, 8 May 2003; *The Independent*, 20 May 2003; *Architects' Journal*, 217 (8 May 2003), 12; *Building*, 268 (30 May 2003), 14; *Building Design*, 1582 (6 June 2003), 7.
2. See also Alan Powers, *Britain: Modern Architecture in History* (London: Reaktion Books, 2007), p. 92.
3. Also lost in the Clandon Park fire were Patrick Gwynne's drawings and model of Studio Cottage, The Homewood, *c* 2003, and five albums compiled by Gwynne of photographs and text titled: (1) 'The Homewood, Esher', (2) 'Interiors, Shops, Restaurants, 1934–1958 & Some Furniture 1938–1970', (3) 'Houses, 1949–1962', (4) 'Houses, 1963–1979' and (5) 'Buildings, 1964–1974'. Digital scans of these albums are in the National Trust Archive.
4. *Building Design*, 1748 (24 November 2006), 1.
5. Where not otherwise credited, all quotes from Gwynne without footnote references in the text of this book are from the National Life Story Collection, Architects' Lives, C467/35, Patrick Gwynne interviewed by Neil Bingham 12 October 1997–6 February 1999. http://sounds.bl.uk/Oral-history/Architects-Lives/021M-C0467X0036XX-0100V0, accessed 14 July 2022.
6. Patrick Gwynne, *Houses by Patrick Gwynne, 1938–1979*, and *Buildings by Patrick Gwynne, 1964–1978*, both privately printed, *c* 1980.
7. Patrick Gwynne, 'The Homewood, Esher, Surrey: Inventory of Loose Furniture Bequeathed to the National Trust', October 1999. This had been preceded by the extensive 'Notes of Meeting held at The Homewood' taken with Gwynne on a walk-about of The Homewood with Christopher Wilk, Keeper of Furniture, Victoria and Albert Museum, and Edward Diestelkamp, National Trust, 21 September 1993, revised 8 October 1993.
8. Peter Aspden, 'The Collections of Stanley J Seeger', *Financial Times*, 24 January 2014.

1 Early life: 1913–30
1. Recipe book and story courtesy Janet Menzies.
2. National Trust, 'Transcript of conversation between Patrick Gwynne, Malcolm Billings and Edward

Diestelkamp', 16 June and 24 July 1995, p. 18.

3   In 2007, four years after Gwynne's death, David Scott and his family took on The Homewood as their home, acting as excellent ambassadors on behalf of the National Trust, supervising guides and welcoming visitors.

4   José Manser, 'Elegance to Divert even Poirot's Gaze', *Building Design*, 1128 (11 June 1993), 11.

5   Sarah C Howard, 'Gwynne, (Alban) Patrick (1913–2003)', *Oxford Dictionary of National Biography*, published online 22 September 2011.

6   Commander Gwynne's lineage was not only connected to wealth through Aberaeron. His father, Alban Gwynne, had married Mary Edith Harford in 1878. She was one of the eight children of John Battersby Harford and Mary Charlotte de Bunsen, who lived in a fine Italianate villa called Falcondale in Cardiganshire. Subsequently, Harford inherited Blaise Castle House near Bristol, a great neo-classical house by the architect William Paty, with a picture room by C R Cockerell and grounds laid out by Humphrey Repton. The estate also boasted the famous picturesque village of Blaise Hamlet by John Nash. In 1915, the three-year-old Patrick, with his family, visited his widowed great-grandmother at Blaise Castle, photographs of the visit appearing in his album (private collection, copy with National Trust). She died four years later, with the house eventually passing to the City of Bristol and Blaise Hamlet to the National Trust.

7   Dix Noonan Webb, Auctioneers, London: Sale 25 September 2008, Lot 1389: six miniature dress medals attributed to Colonel Wensley James Hodson Bond, India Army.

8   The late Victorian house, which Gwynne often derided, was in fact a fine villa that had been owned by the merchant Alexander Constantine Ionides (1840–98), a leading member of the large family that collected old masters and patronised contemporary British art and literature; for example, his brother donated 1,138 pictures, drawing and prints to the Victoria and Albert Museum. Ionides had the interior of his London house in Holland Park rebuilt by the architect Philip Webb as an Arts and Crafts showcase for works by his friends like Whistler, G F Watts, Burne Jones and Walter Crane. Undoubtedly, Homewood must also have been a setting for works from Ionides's large collection. After he died, his widow moved to the Esher house until she sold it to the Gwynnes. See Charles Harvey and Jon Press, 'The Ionides Family and 1 Holland Park', *Decorative Arts Society Journal*, 18, 2–14.

9   The Gwynnes had photographs of Albert Einstein in 1933 standing in the Homewood garden.

10 Harrow School Report, 1929. Private collection, digital scan copy in possession of the National Trust.

2 Becoming an architect: 1930–37

1   Stan Robinson and Brian North Lee, 'John Duke Coleridge and his Bookplates', *Bookplate Journal* (March 1989), 4–17.

2   Dan Cruickshank, 'Trust Worthy', Style Magazine, *Sunday Times*, 4 December 1994, p. 29.

3   In 1935, Berthold Lubetkin painted his modern block of flats, Highpoint in Hampstead, in Stic B. Gwynne used it after the war to repaint The Homewood.

4   In the spring of 1935, Patrick passed the RIBA Intermediate Examination, qualifying him for election as a Student Member of the Institute. Until the Architects Registration Act of 1938, anyone could call themselves an architect. The Act restricted the use of the title 'architect' to those who had qualified under government-approved architectural qualifications. To prepare for his exams, Gwynne did a crammer course on engineering with a man in Gower Street, London.

5   Interview with Patrick Gwynne, 4 September 1994.

6   Interview with Patrick Gwynne, 18 March 1995. This would have been ahead of Mendelsohn's arrival in London. The Nazi-staged boycott of Jewish-owned businesses took place on 1 April 1933, the beginning of their anti-Jewish campaign.

7   Eric Lewenhaupt (1886–1968), with business connections between Sweden and England, was friends with a wide circle including the mystic Alistair Crowley. He translated Swedish books into English, including the memoirs of Count Folke Bernadotte in 1945.

8   Interview with Lasdun by Alan Powers, National Life Story Collection, British Library, C467/32, nd.

9   Gwynne borrowed money from his father to buy the Talbot car as fees for designing The Homewood.

10 Coates biographer Sherban Cantacuzino noted that cooking had become a cult by the 1930s. Coates's friend Morton Shand, the architectural critic and co-founder of the MARS Group, wrote books and articles on food and wine. Wells Coates was an original member of the Half-Hundred supper club, created in 1937 by Jack and Molly Pritchard, the founders of the Isokon Furniture Company and builders of the Lawn Road Flats. Dinners took place in the Pritchards' penthouse flat or in the Isobar. See Sherban Cantacuzino, *Wells Coates: A Monograph* (London: Gordon Fraser, 1978), p. 30.

11 RIBA Drawings Collection, PB885/3(1). Elevations and sketch perspective, 10 Palace Gate, London by Wells Coates, dated 12 March 1937, revised 15 March 1937. The drawing is a printed office copy.

12 Laura Cohen, *The Door to a Secret Room: A Portrait of Wells Coates* (Aldershot: Scholar Press, 1999), p. 125.

13 A third unidentified house interior on Upper Brook Street, Mayfair, possibly dates from this period, noted by Gwynne on the cover text of album 'Interiors, Shops, Restaurants 1934–1958 & Some Furniture 1938–1970', digital copy in National Trust Archive.

3 The Homewood: 1937–39

1   Gwynne also told Alan Powers in an interview, 'it is always very difficult this because I don't like to say that Wells didn't have anything to do with it because he had lots to do with it, but he didn't design it, he had a totally different idea when I said that my father wanted to build a house'. National Life Story Collection, British Library, C467/32, nd.

2   Coates's two principal biographers attribute The Homewood jointly to Gwynne and Coates.

Sherban Cantacuzino, *Wells Coates: A Monograph* (London: Gordon Fraser, 1978), and Elizabeth Darling, *Wells Coates*. (London: RIBA Publishing, 2012).

3   Miscellaneous interviews and correspondence with Patrick Gwynne by the author, 1993; Office for National Statistics, table 502: Housing market, house prices from 1930. The purchase price of an average house in 1938 was approximately £545.

4   *Architectural Review*, 88 (September 1939), 103–16. In the article, The Homewood is credited to 'Patrick Gwynne and Wells Coates, Architects'; a photograph and plans of The Homewood appeared in *A Decade of New Architecture*, ed. by S Giedion (Zurich: Girsberger, 1951), p. 82, attributed to 'WELLS COATES (with P. Gwynne)'; the publication featured contributions submitted by members of CIAM, in which Coates played an important role.

5   National Trust Archive, 'Transcript of conversation between Patrick Gwynne, Malcolm Billings and Edward Diestelkamp', 16 June and 24 July 1995, p. 2.

6   For a fuller description of The Homewood interior, see the guidebook: Neil Bingham, *The Homewood* (London: The National Trust, 2004).

7   Leslie Bilsby, 'A Lifetime's Devotion', *RIBA Journal*, 88 (November 1981), 51–3.

8   Miscellaneous interviews and correspondence with Gwynne by the author, 1993.

9   National Trust Archive, 'The Landscape: a discussion with Mr Gwynne about the history and development of the landscape at The Homewood', 9 October 1993. Gwynne made specific reference to Christopher Tunnard, *Gardens in the Modern Landscape* (London: Architectural Press, 1938).

10 C H Reilly, 'The Year's Work', *Architects' Journal*, 91 (18 January 1940), 89–91.

4   The war and mid-century modern: 1940–59

1   National Trust Archive, 'Transcript of conversation between Patrick Gwynne, Malcolm Billings and Edward Diestelkamp', 16 June and 24 July 1995, p. 14.

2   Undated letter, c 1943–4, from Gwynne to Gladys Gwynne, courtesy of George Cruddas.

3   National Trust Archive, 'The Landscape: a discussion with Mr Gwynne about the history and development of the landscape at The Homewood', 9 October 1993.

4   RIBA, RIBA Nomination Papers, 'Patrick Gwynne', 1946.

5   *Architect and Building News*, 195 (21 January 1949), 49–51; *Architectural Design*, 19 (May 1949), 121.

6   *Architect and Building News* (17 April 1952), 453–6.

7   Interview with Tanya House, née Bilsby, 29 October 2019.

8   *Eric Lyons and Span*, ed. by B Simms (London: RIBA Publishing, 2006), including N Bingham, 'The Architect in Society: Eric Lyons, his circle and his values', pp. 1–21.

9   *Architectural Review*, 117 (April 1955), 258–9.

10 *Ideal Home and Gardening*, 69 (February 1954), 40–1.

11 *House and Garden*, 10 (December 1955), 64–7.

12 To achieve the spectrum of painted

colours for the pavilion tents, Gwynne may well have used Wilhelm Ostwald's colour plates. The Crescent was dismantled after the following summer season, 1952, by which time the colours were overpainted in pink.

13 *Architect and Building News*, 199 (15 June 1951), 700.
14 *Architectural Design*, 28 (July 1958), 291.
15 *Architect & Building News*, 204 (26 November 1953), 638–41.
16 Interviews with Gwynne, 4–5 April 1994.
17 *Architect and Building News*, 204 (3 December 1953), 699.
18 National Trust Archive: Gwynne Album 'Interiors Shops Restaurants 1934–1958'.
19 *Architect and Building News*, 28 (22 December 1955), 800–1.
20 *Ideal Home and Gardening*, 81 (August 1960), 22–6.
21 Alice Hope, *Town Houses* (London: Batsford, 1964), pp. 83–5.
22 *Ideal Home and Gardening*, 80 (December 1959), 66–71.
23 Fay Sweet, 'All Mod Cons,' *Independent on Sunday*, 13 August 2000, colour supplement, pp. 26–7; Alan Powers, 'Modern Classic: The Firs', *Grand Designs* (March 2007), 100–5.
24 P Gwynne, *Houses by Patrick Gwynne, 1938–1979*, privately printed, c 1980.
25 *Home* (July–August 1963), 32–5.
26 Interview with Tony Salmon, 19 February 2015.
27 Ibid.
28 Mark Girouard, 'A Change from Neo-Georgian: Witley Park, near Godalming', *Country Life*, 134 (19 December 1963), 1693–5; also *Architectural Review*, 133 (Mar 1963), 169–73.
29 'The Witley Park Estate', sales document, Weller Eggar and John D Wood and Co, auctioneers, for 26 July 1973, p. 7.

5 The art of living: 1960–84

1 *Architectural Review*, 136 (October 1964), 245–51.
2 *Building Design*, 942 (23 June 1989), 1; *Building Design*, 977 (16 March 1990), 1.
3 Letter from Donald Bodley to Gwynne, 16 July 1965. RIBA Archive and Manuscripts Collection, GWP/1. The architects unceremoniously terminated were the cinema specialists Gavin Paterson & Son of Glasgow.
4 Nikolaus Pevsner and David Neave, *Yorkshire: York and the East Riding* (London: Yale University Press, 1995), p. 198.
5 Letter from Gwynne to the author, 10 April 2000.
6 National Trust Archive: digital copy of Patrick Gwynne, 'Buildings, 1964–1979', unpublished.
7 Gwynne claimed that the south pavilion of the Burtonwood M62 station was demolished because the facilities were no longer required when Liverpool went into a slump.
8 Interview with Gwynne, 24 April 1992.
9 The Courtyard House model, accompanied by relevant drawings, is part of the Gwynne archive at the RIBA.
10 Interview with Bob King, 8 April 2019.
12 Letters, John F Lewis, Housing Editor, *Ideal Home*, to Kenneth Knowles, 29 December 1972 and Knowles to Lewis, 28 January 1973 (in author's possession). Knowles lived in Ananda for only a few years. The next occupant was Josh Manches, a Harley Street

dentist, who rehired King to make changes to the house, converting the garage into a bedroom, adding a detached garage with a shaped entrance profile, a swimming pool, and, drastic but cosmetic and in its way beautiful, wrapping of the dark brick of the top first-floor exterior with white vinyl siding, a complete contrast to the dark brick which remained below.

12 Interview with Gwynne, 3 October 1993.
13 Anne Sinai, *Reach for the Top: The Turbulent Life of Laurence Harvey* (Lanham, MD and Oxford: Scarecrow Press, 2003).
14 Interview with Paulene Stone, 24 April 2017.
15 Paulene Stone, *One Tear is Enough: My Life with Laurence Harvey* (London: Michael Joseph, 1975), pp. 154–5.
16 *Building Design*, 775 (21 February 1986), 18.
17 RIBA Drawings Collection, PB627/7(1–11).
18 Interview with Vivien Griffiths, 15 November 2018.
19 Correspondence from Vivien Griffiths to author, 21 August 2019.

6 The Homewood: 1940–2003

1 *Ideal Home and Gardening*, 53.6 (June 1946). The cover illustration is a rather bizarre illustration showing exotic birds flying over the house while the tiny dapper figure of Gwynne is seen below leaning out of a window and Babs reclines on the patio in her brother's prized Bruno Mathsson chaise longue. Perhaps the surreal tone of the image was to be expected, as its painter was Ithell Colquhoun (1906–88), a member of the 1930s British Surrealist Group who had been expelled for her esoteric beliefs and paintings referencing sex and gender.

2 For a short time after the war, Gwynne had an office on Great Smith Street, London, but did not use it.
3 Interviews with Bob King, 5 November 2018 and 8 April 2019.
4 Ibid.
5 Elvine (Cottrell) Baird, correspondence with author, 12 March 2020.
6 Ibid.
7 Recorded interview with Cottrell by David Scott at The Homewood, 9 October 2018.
8 Interview with Tony Salmon, 19 February 2015.
9 This little model now entertains visitors to the V&A/RIBA Architecture Gallery of the Victoria and Albert Museum.
10 When Mrs Wright retired, she moved to a care home where Gwynne would often visit her. For a short time after Mrs Wright left, Gwynne had a young husband and wife who assisted him and lived in the staff flat.
11 Correspondence with Elvine Cottrell, 12 March 2020.
12 National Trust Archive: Transcript of conversation between Patrick Gwynne, Malcolm Billings and Edward Diestelkamp, 16 June and 24 July 1995, pp. 21–2.
13 Interview with Raymond Menzies, 16 January 2019.
14 See *Radio Times*, 1478 (7 March 1952), p. 23.
15 Recorded interview with Cottrell by David Scott at The Homewood, 9 October 2018; Correspondence with Bernard Jay and author, 12 November and 8 December 2019. Jay had been house manager at York and was 21 years old at the time. He went on to a distinguished career in actor and theatre

management in America and South Africa, including personal manager to the famous drag queen Divine.

16 National Trust Archive: Transcript of conversation between Patrick Gwynne, Malcolm Billings and Edward Diestelkamp, 16 June and 24 July 1995, p. 33.

17 Neil Bingham, 'The Homewood, Surrey: The Home of Mr Patrick Gwynne,' *Country Life*, 87 (22 July 1993), 84–7.

18 In 1948, a pair of photographs emphasising these built-in wall displays appeared in Frederick Gibberd's slim volume *Built-In Furniture in Great Britain*, with text in English and French (London: Alec Tiranti). A view of the living room also appeared in the popular little book by Lionel Brett, *The Things We See: Houses* (Drayton, Middx: Penguin Books, 1947) p. 48. Brett's prejudices for architects who were his friends, and those who were not, emerged in his caption: 'the gleaming surfaces and precise detailing still dictate too cruelly how you shall live.' This image appears to have reached a wide audience because Gwynne said that children or their parents commented that they recognised the house from the book which was probably on many school library shelves. (National Trust Archive: Transcript of conversation between Patrick Gwynne, Malcolm Billings and Edward Diestelkamp, 16 June and 24 July 1995, p. 9).

19 Knapp had installed similar panels on the concourse façade of Sir Frederick Gibberd's Terminal Building at Heathrow Airport in 1959.

20 Lady Gibberd visited Gwynne at The Homewood on 15 May 1992 at the invitation of the author. The pair set up a correspondence in which Gwynne wrote to her 'I think you are quite right to nudge me regarding the future of The Homewood.' (Letter from Gwynne to Lady Gibberd, 17 July 1992, copy in author's possession).

21 'Though I personally dislike the big Stephan [sic] Knapp enamel on the garden front, I would be prepared to accept that and his dining room hatch as works of art. But again they are typically '60s in character, and again tend to destroy the '30s feel of the house. Oh for some Marion Dorn carpets or Eileen Grey screen!' National Trust Memorandum from Gervase Jackson-Stops, Architectural Advisor, to Martin Drury, Deputy Director-General, 16 November 1993.

22 The film sequence with Gwynne and The Homewood in the documentary *Treasures in Trust* (1995) is available at www.youtube.com/watch?v=KzIOrMItd9s, accessed 4 April 2022.

23 National Trust Archive: 'The Future of The Homewood: A statement by Patrick Gwynne concerning his proposed bequest of The Homewood, Esher, to the National Trust', August 1996.

24 Interview with Gwynne, 4 September 1994.

25 John Allan, 'Architect's account', in Elain Harwood, 'Homewood bound: Lifetime Achievement', *Architects' Journal*, 219 (1 April 2004), 30–9.

26 Interview with John Allan and Fiona Lamb, 15 March 2019.

27 National Trust Archive: Patrick Gwynne, 'The Homewood Esher: Garden Notes by Patrick Gwynne', August 1999.

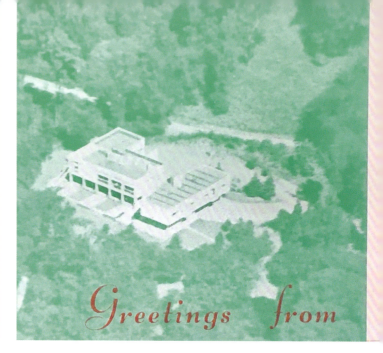

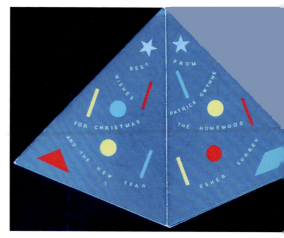

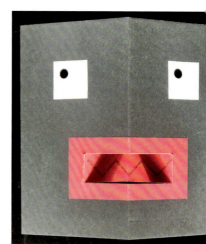

List of works

Substantially altered or partly demolished = *
Demolished = **
Unbuilt projects = ***
Bold type indicates works profiled in this book

1935
Lawn Road Flats
London
Architect: Wells Coates
Client: Jack and Molly Pritchard/
Isokon Ltd
Entrance desk
Listed at grade I

1935
Embassy Court
King's Parade, Brighton
Architect: Wells Coates
Client: Maddox Properties Ltd
Detailing
Listed at grade II*

1935
Studio flat**
18 Yeoman's Row, London
Architect and client: Wells Coates
Supervising architect

1937
Shipwrights
Benfleet Road, Benfleet, Essex
Architect: Wells Coates
Client: John Wyborn
Supervising architect
Listed at grade II*

1937–9
10 Palace Gate
Kensington, London
Architect: Wells Coates
Client: Ten Palace Gate Ltd (Randal Bell)
Detailing
Listed at grade II*

1937
Interior, Mews House**
Near Marble Arch, London
Client: Peter Klaus von Krauschen

1937
Interior, Bruton Street★★
Mayfair, London
Client: Dr Langdale Clarke

1937–8
The Homewood
Portsmouth Road, Esher, Surrey
Client: Commander and Mrs
A L Gwynne
Listed at grade II
Architectural Review, 88 (Sep 1939), 103–16
Ideal Home, 53 (Jun 1946), 22–33
Country Life, 187 (22 Jul 1993), 84–7
Neil Bingham, 'The Houses of Patrick Gwynne', Twentieth Century Architecture, 4 (2000), 30–44

1949
EMG Shop★★
6 Newman St, Marylebone, London
Client: EMG Handmade Gramophones Ltd
Architect and Building News, 195 (21 Jan 1949), 49–51
Architectural Design, 19 (May 1949), 121
Architects' Journal, 109 (9 Jun 1949), 523–6

1949
25 Dawson Place, assists Denys Lasdun (fitments)★★
Notting Hill, London
Architect and Building News, 196 (4 Nov 1949), 448–52

1949–54
115 Blackheath Park★★
Blackheath, London
Client: Leslie Bilsby
Demolished 1966

Architectural Review, 117 (Apr 1955), 258–9
Design (Apr 1955), 40–1
Architect and Building News, 207 (16 Jun 1955), 724–8
Ideal Home, 81 (Jul 1955), 64–8
Bingham, 'The Houses of Patrick Gwynne', 32–3

1950
Flat interior, including a birdcage for a parrot★★
4 Upper Brook Street, Mayfair, London
Client: Peter Claas

1950
Competition design for restaurant, second prize★★★
South Bank, London
Client: 1951 Festival of Britain

1951
Crescent Restaurant★★
Battersea Park, London
Client: 1951 Festival of Britain
Country Life, 109 (15 Jun 1951), 1898–1902

1952
House interior with gramophone cabinet★★
Campden Hill Road, Kensington, London
Client: Cyril Sweett

1952
Shop for Supreme Radio★★
Silver Street, Edmonton, London
Architect and Building News, 201 (17 Apr 1952), 453–7

LIST OF WORKS

Gwynne's model of a conjectural design for a curved-roof bungalow appeared in *Ideal Home* magazine in 1954

1953
Stand for Royal Institute of Chartered Surveyors, Building Exhibition**
Olympia, London
Architect and Building News, 204 (3 Dec 1953), 699

1953
Freeman, Hardy and Willis shoe shop**
154 Rushey Green, Catford, London
Client: Charles Clore
Architect and Building News, 204 (26 Nov 1953), 637–41

1954
Design for a curved-roof bungalow for *Ideal Home* magazine***
Ideal Home, 69 (Feb 1954), 40–1

1954
Music Studio, The White House**
Millfield Place, Highgate, London
Client: Clifford Curzon
Architect and Building News, 207 (9 Jun 1955), 679–83
House and Garden, 10 (Dec 1955), 64–7

1955
Butterwalk Restaurant and Café**
The Butterwalk, Dartmouth, Devon

1955
Ox on the Roof Restaurant**
Chelsea, London
Architect and Building News, 208 (22 Dec 1955), 800–1
Architectural Design, 26 (Feb 1956), 67

c 1955
Gardener's Cottage, Wood Farm**
Pledgdon Green, Henham, Essex
Client: Noreen Cruddas

135

1956
Mayfair Colour Centre London★★
Architect and Building News, 209 (12 Apr 1956), 380

1957
Competition design for a Canadian House★★★
Client: Canadian Wood Association

c 1957
Offices and computer display window★★
110 St Martin's Lane, Westminster, London
Client: London Press Exchange

1958
Offices, Bedford Row★★
Holborn, London
Client: Cyril Sweett and Partners, quantity surveyors
Architectural Design, 208 (Jul 1958), 291

1958
31 Glenferness Avenue★
Bournemouth, Dorset
Client: Jack Hawkins (for mother-in-law, Mrs Beadle)
Builder, 198 (18 Mar 1960), 545–7
Ideal Home, 8 (Aug 1960), 22–6
Bingham, 'The Houses of Patrick Gwynne', 33

1958
Music room, Chestnut Lodge
Old Common Road, Cobham, Surrey

1958–59
Sunday Times Hampton Site Competition design for the National Gallery★★★
Trafalgar Square, London

1959
The Firs
24 Spaniards End, Hampstead, London
Client: Otto and Marion Edler
Listed at grade II
Ideal Home, 80 (Dec 1959), 66–71
Builder, 198 (19 Feb 1960), 356–9
Bingham, 'The Houses of Patrick Gwynne', 33–4

1959–60
Fairoaks, Mulberry, Woodlands and Junipers★★
Coombe Hill Road, Kingston upon Thames
Client: Kenneth Monk
Demolished except Woodlands
Architectural Review, 129 (Mar 1961), 176–7
Alice Hope, *Town Houses* (London: Batsford, 1963), pp. 83–5
Bingham, 'The Houses of Patrick Gwynne', 34–5

c 1960
Offices Chancery Lane★★
London
Client: Monk and Dunstone, quantity surveyors
Gwynne later designed another office for the practice in Hobart Place

LIST OF WORKS

1960
Past Field
9 Rotherfield Road, Henley-on-Thames, Oxfordshire
Client: Dr and Mrs A Salmon (addition, 1966)
Listed at grade II
House and Garden, Supplement, 172 (Jun 1963), 19
Penelope Whiting, *New Houses* (London: Architectural Press, 1964), pp. 118–22
Bingham, 'The Houses of Patrick Gwynne', 34

1960
Courtyard House★★★
Blackheath, London
Client: Leslie Bilsby

1961
4 Beechworth Close
Hampstead, London
Client: Max and Anne Bruh
Listed at grade II
Home (Jul–Aug 1963), 32–5
Bingham, 'The Houses of Patrick Gwynne', 35

1961
Westwood Road★★★
Windlesham, Surrey
Client: Laurence Harvey

c 1962
Civic Hall, Guildford, competition★★★

1962
Witley Park
Brook, Godalming, Surrey
Client: Gerald and Sybil Bentall
Architectural Review, 133 (Mar 1963), 169–73

Country Life, 134 (19 Dec 1963), 1693–5
Bingham, 'The Houses of Patrick Gwynne', 36

1963
3 Beechworth Close★
Hampstead, London
Client: Mr and Mrs Hornung
Bingham, 'The Houses of Patrick Gwynne', 35–6

c 1963
Office, Bentall's Department Store★★
Kingston upon Thames, Surrey
Client: Gerald Bentall

1964
Serpentine Restaurant★★
Hyde Park, London
Client: Charles Forte/Ministry of Public Buildings and Works
Extensions 1965 and 1971
Demolished 1990
Architect and Building News, 224, 715
Builder, 205 (8 Nov 1963), 935–6
Architects' Journal, 139 (17 Jun 1964), 1338
Architect and Building News, 225 (24 Jun 1964), 1125–8
Concrete Quarterly, 62 (Jul–Sep 1964), 7–9
Architectural Review, 136 (Oct 1964), 245–51
Architects' Journal, 154 (13 Oct 1971), 825–6

1964
Heston Motor Services Area★★★
M4, London

c 1965
Studio for Stefan Knapp

c 1965
Studio Cottage, The Homewood
Interior alterations

1965
The Dell Restaurant
Hyde Park, London
Client: Charles Forte/Ministry of Public Buildings and Works
Listed at grade II*
The Builder, 209 (17 Sep 1965), 594–6

1965
Grovewood★★
West Drive, Wentworth Estate, Surrey
Client: David and Jean Shaw
Demolished c 1993
Ideal Home, 92 (Oct 1966), 70–3
Joyce Lowrie, *House and Garden: Modern Houses in Town and Country* (London and Glasgow: Collins, 1974), p. 41
Bingham, 'The Houses of Patrick Gwynne', 39

1966
Hotel extension, The Phoenicia★★★
Floriana, Malta

1967
Theatre Royal, York, extension and renovation
Client: Theatre Royal Trustees/York City Council
Listed at grade II*
Architectural Review, 144 (Sep 1968), 187–91
Design (Nov 1968), 56–9
Architects' Journal, 148 (4 Dec 1968), 1335–42
Building, 216 (10 Jan 1969), 85–9
Architect and Building News, 4 (9 Oct 1969), 93–5 and (6 Nov 1969), 127–8

1968
Vista Point
Telgħet ix-Xemxija, St Paul's Bay, Malta
Client: Kenneth Monk
Bingham, 'The Houses of Patrick Gwynne', 39–40

1968
Seaside House★★★
Mellieħa Bay, Malta
Client: Mr and Mrs Edwards

c 1968
Consultation work with Leslie Bilsby and Span architect Eric Lyons on New Ash Green, Kent

1969
Civic hall, Whitehaven, Cumbria, competition★★★

1969
10 Blackheath Park
Blackheath, London
Client: Leslie Bilsby
Listed at grade II
House and Garden, 25 (Dec 1970–Jan 1971), 50–3
Ideal Home, 102 (Nov 1971), 47–51
Joyce Lowrie, *House and Garden: Modern Houses in Town and Country* (London and Glasgow: Collins, 1974), p. 44
Bingham, 'The Houses of Patrick Gwynne', 37–8

1970
Vista Point
21 Tamarisk Way, Angmering-on-Sea, Sussex
Client: Kenneth and Molly Monk
Listed at grade II

LIST OF WORKS

1970
Hart Medical Surgery*
York Road, Henley-on-Thames, Oxfordshire
Client: NHS/ A Salmon
Architects' Journal, 154 (8 Sep 1971), 502–3

1971
Parliamentary Offices, Bridge Street, Whitehall, competition***

1971
Ananda**
Meadway, Esher, Surrey
Client: Kenneth and Muriel Knowles
Demolished c 2000
Bingham, 'The Houses of Patrick Gwynne', 40

1971
3 Kidderpore Avenue (alterations and additions)*
Hampstead, London
Client: Laurence Harvey and Paulene Stone
Bingham, 'The Houses of Patrick Gwynne', 40–1

1971
Two Houses***
Saint-Paul-de-Vence, France
Client: Laurence Harvey and Leslie Bricusse

1972
House, Malibu Beach***
California, USA
Client: Laurence Harvey

1972
Enclosed swimming pool for a house, Hampstead, London

1973
House in France, for Leslie Bilsby***

1973
House, Abinger Common***
Surrey
Client: a brick company director

1973
Ryde Farm, conversion of barn to a house***
Ripley, Surrey
Client: Sir Charles Forte

1974
Burtonwood Motorway Services Area*
M62, near Warrington, Cheshire
Client: Charles Forte
One of two buildings demolished

1974
House for a hilltop***

1974
House, Blackheath, London***
Client: Leslie Bilsby

1975
Restaurant, Saffa Park*
Dubai, United Arab Emirates

1975
Chigwell Motorway Services Area***
M11, Essex

1975
Restaurant and pub, Ampney Crucis, Gloucestershire***

139

1976
Apartment and office building, Abu Dhabi, United Arab Emirates, with Michael Manser, architect***

1978
Fairmile Hotel, extension*
Cobham, Surrey
Client: Charles Forte

1979
22 Parkgate
Blackheath, London
Client: Leslie Bilsby
Bingham, 'The Houses of Patrick Gwynne', 38–9

1979
Enclosure for swimming pool for a house, Lindford, Hampshire

c 1980
Sauna complex, Hays Mews**
Westminster, London
Client: Stanley J Seeger

1981
Squash Court
Sutton Place, Surrey
Client: Stanley J Seeger

1981
Top flat, 49 Berkeley Square**
London
Client: Stanley J Seeger

1981
Flat 3, 26 St James's Place**
Westminster, London
Client: Stanley J Seeger

1982
Competition design for extension to the National Gallery**
Trafalgar Square, London

1984
Winterdown
Portsmouth Road, Esher
Client: Robin and Georgina Fawcett
Bingham, 'The Houses of Patrick Gwynne', 41–2

1986
Pyefleet, apartment block**
Angmering-on-Sea, Tamarisk Way, West Sussex

1986
Shops and offices**
1–13 Blackheath Village, London
Building Design, 775 (21 Feb 1986), 18

1999–2000
2 South Parade, addition of bedroom and studio flat
Bedford Park, London
Client: Vivien Griffiths
Listed grade II

1994–2003
Conservation and repair of The Homewood
Client: The National Trust (with Avanti Architects)
Architects' Journal, 219 (1 Apr 2004), 30–9

2003
Studio Cottage, The Homewood (plan outline only)
Esher, Surrey

Plans for houses and buildings

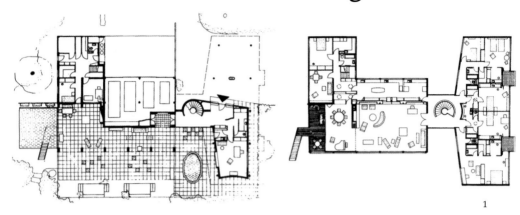

1

2

3

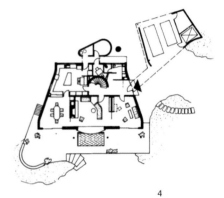

4

Houses
Plans drawn by Gwynne, taken from his *Houses by Patrick Gwynne, 1938–1979*, self-printed, c 1980
(n.b. = not built)

1 1938 The Homewood, : (left) ground and (right) first floor (with 1970s interior arrangement)
2 1949 115 Blackheath Park, London
3 1958 31 Glenferness Avenue, Bournemouth
4 1959 24 Spaniards End, London
5 1960 Model house for Blackheath (n.b.)
6 1960 Coombe Hill Road, London

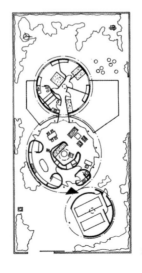

5

6

141

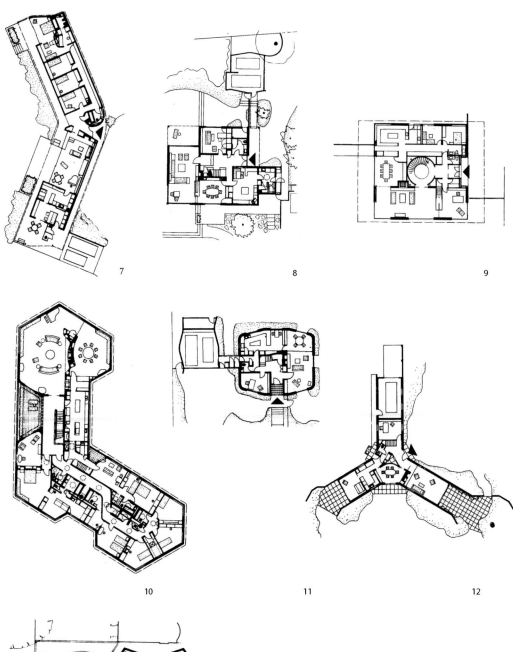

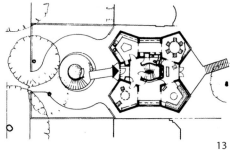

7 1960 9 Rotherfield Road, Henley-on-Thames
8 1961 4 Beechworth Close, London
9 1961 Westwood Road, Windlesham (n.b.)
10 1962 Witley Park, Godalming
11 1963 3 Beechworth Close, London
12 1965 West Drive, Wentworth Estate
13 1969 10 Blackheath Park, London

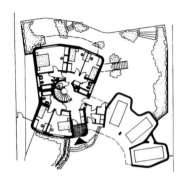

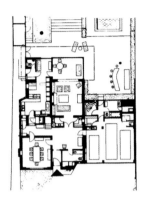

14

15

16

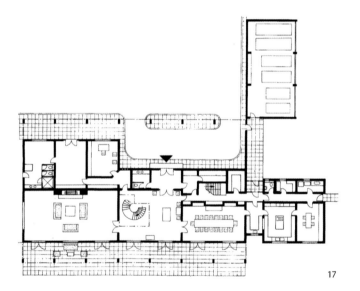

17

18

14 1970 21 Tamarisk Way, Angmering-on-Sea
15 1971 Meadway, Esher
16 1971 3 Kidderpore Avenue, London
17 1973 Ryde Farm, Ripley (n.b.)
18 1972 Malibu Beach, California (n.b.)
19 1971 Saint-Paul-de-Vence, France (n.b.)
20 1979 22 Parkgate, London

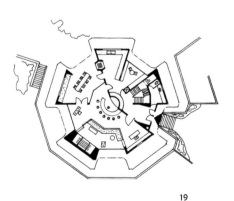

19

20

143

Buildings

1 1964 Serpentine Restaurant, London
2 1964 Heston Motor Services Area, M4 (n.b.)
3 1965 The Dell Restaurant, London
4 1966 Phoenicia Hotel, Malta (n.b.)

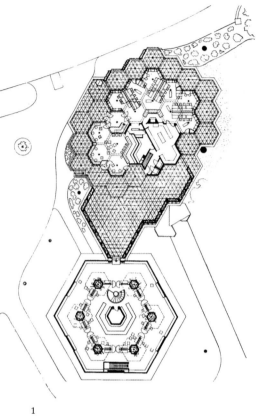

1

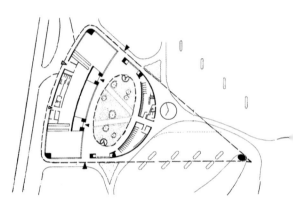

2

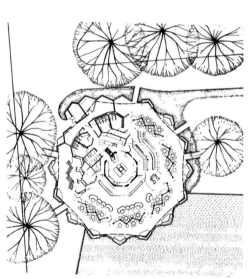

3

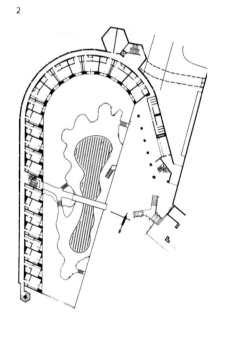

4

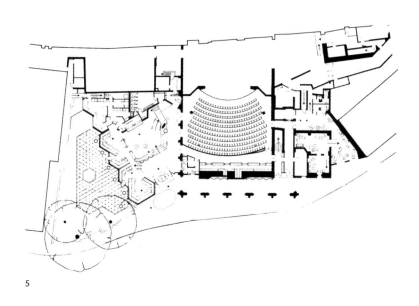

5

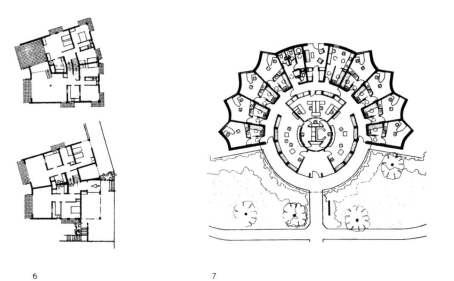

6 7

5 1967 Theatre Royal, York
6 1968 Apartments, St Paul's Bay, Malta
7 1970 Surgery, York Road, Henley-on-Thames

145

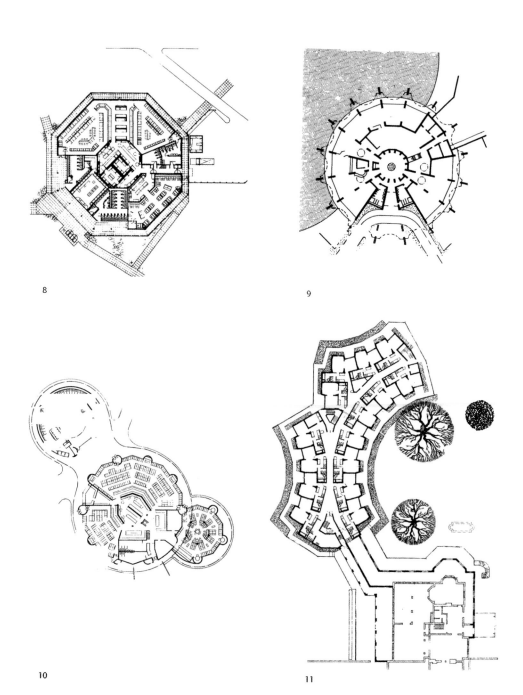

8 1974 Burtonwood Motorway Services Area, M62
9 1975 Restaurant, Saffa Park, Dubai
10 1975 Chigwell Motorway Services Area, M11 (n.b.)
11 1978 Fairmile Hotel, Cobham (n.b.)

The Twentieth Century Society

Without the Twentieth Century Society an entire chapter of Britain's recent history was to have been lost. It was alert when others slept. It is still crucial!
SIMON JENKINS, WRITER, HISTORIAN, JOURNALIST

The Twentieth Century Society campaigns for the preservation of architecture and design in Britain from 1914 onwards and is a membership organisation which you are warmly invited to join and support.

The architecture of the twentieth century has shaped our world and must be part of our future; it includes bold, controversial, and often experimental buildings that range from the playful Deco of seaside villas to the Brutalist concrete of London's Hayward Gallery. The Twentieth Century Society produces many publications of its own to increase knowledge and understanding of this exciting range of work. The Twentieth Century Architects series has enabled the Society to extend its reach through partnership, initially with RIBA Publishing and now with Historic England, contributing the contacts and expertise needed to create enjoyable and accessible introductions to the work of architects who deserve more attention. In the process, the books contribute to the work of protecting buildings from demolition or disfigurement.

We propose buildings for listing, advise on restoration and help to find new uses for buildings threatened with demolition. Join the Twentieth Century Society and not only will you help to protect these modern treasures, you will also gain an unrivalled insight, through our magazine, journal and events programme, into the ground-breaking architecture and design that helped to shape the century.

For further details and to join online, see www.c20society.org.uk

CATHERINE CROFT
DIRECTOR

Other titles in the series

Ahrends, Burton and Koralek
Kenneth Powell
Apr 2012
978-1-85946-166-2

Aldington, Craig and Collinge
Alan Powers
Nov 2009 (out of print)
978-1-85946-302-4

Arup Associates
Kenneth Powell
Jun 2018
978-1-84802-367-3

Stephen Dykes Bower
Anthony Symondson
Dec 2011
978-1-85946-398-7

Chamberlin, Powell & Bon
Elain Harwood
Nov 2011
978-1-85694-397-0

Edward Cullinan Architects
Kenneth Powell
??? 2022
978-1-80207-755-1

Wells Coates
Elizabeth Darling
Jul 2012
978-1-85946-437-3

Frederick Gibberd
Christine Hui Lan Manley
Sep 2017
978-1-84802-273-7

Howell Killick Partridge & Amis
Geraint Franklin
Jun 2017
978-1-84802-275-1

McMorran & Whitby
Edward Denison
Oct 2009
978-1-85946-320-8

John Madin
Alan Clawley
Mar 2011
978-1-85946-367-3

Robert Maguire & Keith Murray
Gerald Adler
Mar 2012
978-1-85946-165-5

Leonard Manasseh & Partners
Timothy Brittain-Catlin
Dec 2010
978-1-85946-368-0

John Outram
Geraint Franklin
Apr 2022
978-1-84802-558-5

Peter Moro and Partners
Alistair Fair
Aug 2021
978-1-80085-651-6

Powell & Moya
Kenneth Powell
Apr 2009
978-1-85946-303-1

Herbert Rowse
Iain Jackson, Simon Pepper and Peter Richmond
Jun 2019
978-1-84802-549-3

Ryder and Yates
Rutter Caroll
Apr 2009
978-1-85946-266-9

Alison and Peter Smithson
Mark Crinson
Jun 2018
978-1-84802-352-9

F X Velarde
Dominic Wilkinson and Andrew Crompton
Oct 2020
978-1-78962-814-2

Forthcoming titles

Architects' Co-Partnership
Alan Powers

Ralph Erskine
Elain Harwood

Ernö Goldfinger
Elain Harwood and Alan Powers

Berthold Lubetkin
John Allan

William Whitfield
Roland Jeffery

Peter Womersley
Neil Jackson

Illustration credits

The author and publisher have made every effort to contact copyright holders and will be happy to correct, in subsequent editions, any errors or omissions that are brought to their attention.

Architectural Press Archive / RIBA Collections
32 (top), 51 (top), 60, 71 (top), 80, 81, 83, 104 (top)

Brian Duffy / Brian Duffy Archive Ltd
103

Country Life (Mark Fiennes)
xv, 24

Elain Harwood
12

George Cruddas
85

Gwynne family
3, 7, 9 (top and bottom), 10

Historic England (James O. Davies)
ii, vi, viii, x, 20, 64, 65, 67, 72, 78–9, 89, 92, 96, 99

Historic England Archive
xvi, 5

National Portrait Gallery
19

National Trust (James O. Davies)
front cover

Neil Bingham
Back cover, xiii, 107, 112, 118, 120, 122

Paulene Stone
104 (bottom)

Raymond Menzies
14, 21, 22, 27, 28, 29, 30, 32, 34, 41, 43, 49, 51 (bottom), 53, 56, 57, 58, 61, 62, 87, 100, 116, 124, 132

RIBA Collections
31, 36, 38, 45, 54, 69, 71, 74, 84, 90–1, 95, 97, 108, 110

Tanya House
46, 47

Index

Illustrations are indicated by page numbers in **bold**.

Aalto, Alvar 13
Aberaeraon, Wales 1–2, 25, 66
Abinger Common, Surrey (house) 105, 138
Abu Dhabi 140
Allan, John 61, 122–3
Amersham, High and Over **xvi**, 8, 92
Ampney Crucis, Gloucestershire, restaurant and pub 105, 139
Ananda House, Meadway, Esher, Surrey xi, 98–9, **101**, 105, 113, 139, **143**
Angmering-on-Sea
  Tamarisk Way Pyefleet apartments, 108, 140
  Vista Point 88, **89**, **90–1**, 92, 108, 138, **143**
Architect and Building News 50, 52
Architects' Journal 13
Architects Registration Act (1938) 127n4
Architectural Design 52
Architectural Review 6, 13, 26, 35, 37, 69, 76, 108
Arcon 17, 45, 46
Art Deco 17
Assiniboia, Saskatchewan, Canada 40
Association of House Builders 66
Avanti Architects 61, 122–3

Bacon, Francis 106
Bailey, David 102
Baird, James 5–6
Baker, Sir Herbert 6
Baldwin, Ted 63, 114
Barcelona Pavilion 30
Bauhaus 17, 37
Beadle, Mrs 55, 57, 136
Beatrice of Saxe-Coburg and Gotha, Princess 6
Bedford Row, Holborn 52, 136
Beechworth Close, no.3, London 64, 137, **142**
Beechworth Close, no.4, London 61–3, **64**, **65**, 137, **142**
Benfleet, Shipwrights, 20, **20**, 28, 133
Bentall, Gerald 68, 69, 70, 137
Bentall's department store, Kingston upon Thames 68, 70, 137
Berkeley Square, no.49, London 106, 140
Berlin 16
Bertoia, Harry 111
Best Overend, Acheson 17
Bianchi, Manuel 40
Bilsby, Alexandra 95
Bilsby, Leslie xii, 33, 35, 44–5, 55, 93–6, 107–8, 114, 138, 139
Blackheath 'Courtyard House' xii, 93, **95**, 114, 129n9, 130n9, 139, 141

Blackheath Park, no.10, London **vi**, **viii**, 93, **96**, **97**, 138, **142**
Blackheath Park, no.115, London 45–6, **45**, **46**, **47**, 134, **141**
Blackheath Village, nos.1–3, London 107–8, 140
Bodley, Donald 77, 81
Bond, Wilhelmina (Aunt Mina) 4, 26, 33
Bournemouth, 31 Glenferness Avenue 55, 57, **58**, 136, **141**
Brett, Lionel 131n18
Breuer, Marcel 12
Bricusse, Leslie 105, 139
Brighton, Embassy Court 16, 133
British Library, National Life Stories xii
Brown, Lady (Carol) xii, 70
Brown, Mather 1
Brown, Sir Raymond 70
Bruh, Max and Anne 61, 63, 64, 137
Brussels World Fair (1958) xii
Brutalism xi, 68
Bruton Street, London **22**, 23, 134
Buff, Conrad 101
Building Design xii, 76
Burtonwood Motorway Services Area 82–4, **84**, 129n7, 139, **146**

151

Butterwalk Restaurant and Coffee Bar, Dartmouth, 54–5, **56**, 135

Caine, Sir Michael 103
Campden Hill Road, London 134
Canadian Wood Association, competition house **38**, 54, 136
Candela, Félix 83
Cantacuzino, Sherban 76
Carson, Violet 114
Casson, Sir Hugh xiv, 48
Catford, Freeman, Hardy and Willis 52, **54**, 135
Cator Estate 45
Chancery Lane, London 52, 136
Chelsea, Ox on the Roof restaurant 55, **57**, 135
Chermayeff, Serge, 12, 26
Chestnut Lodge, Cobham 48, **49**, 136
Chigwell Motorway Services Area 84, 139, **146**
Claas, Peter 48, 50, 134
Clandon Park, Surrey, fire xi–xii, xii, 125n3
Clarke, Dr Langdale, 22, 23, 134
Clore, Charles 52, 135
Coates, Brian 15–16
Coates, Marion 16
Coates, Wells 12, 16–19, **19**, 20, 23, 25–6, 33, 35, 42, 76, 113, 127n10, 127–8n2, 133
Cobham
    Chestnut Lodge 48, **49**, 136
    Fairmile Hotel 86, 140, **146**
Cohen, B and Sons 13, **15**

Cole, E K, Limited (ECKO) 17, 20
Coleridge, John Duke 11
Coleridge, Paul Humphrey 11
Coleridge and Jennings 11–12, **12**
Collins, Dame Joan 103, 105
computers 53
Coastal Chambers, Elizabeth Street 17
Cone, Christopher 105–6
Congrès Internationaux d'Architecture Moderne 17
Connell, Amyas **xvi**, 8
Connell, Ward and Lucas 8, 12
Coombe Hill Road, Kingston upon Thames 59, **60**, 64, 136, **141**
Cottrell, Elvine 112–13, 115
Country Life 68, 70, 117
Courtyard House (model) Blackheath, London xii, 93, **95**, 114, 129n9, 130n9, 139, **141**
Crescent Restaurant, Festival Pleasure Gardens, Battersea 48, 50, **51**, 55, 73, 134
Cruddas, George 105, 106, 112, 121–2
Cruddas, William 111
Cunningham, Ivor 95
Curzon, Sir Clifford 48, 49
Curzon music studio 46, 48, **49**, 135

Daily Mail Ideal Home Exhibition 25
Dartmouth, Butterwalk Restaurant and Coffee Bar 54–5, **56**, 135
Davis Jr, Sammy 101

Dawson Place, London 25, 134
Dell and Wainwright 26, 108
Dell Restaurant, Hyde Park, London viii–ix, 76–7, **77**, 78–9, 138, **144**
demolitions xi, 59, 75–6, 93–4, 98
Director, The 52
Donat, John 74, 76
dual turntable gramophone 53
Dubai, Saffa Park 84–6, **85**, 139, **146**
Dudley Ward, Freda 6
Dugdale, Michael 108
Dunkley, Christopher 121

ECKO 17, 20
Edler, Otto 59
Edmonton, Supreme Radio 43–4, **44**, 134
Edward, Prince of Wales 6
Eindhoven, Netherlands 42
Einstein, Albert 6 126n9
Embassy Court, Brighton 16, 133
Emberton, Joseph 12
EMG Handmade Gramophones Ltd 17, 42–3, **43**, 52, 134
Esher, Ananda xi, 98–9, **101**, 105, 113, 139, **143**
Esher, see Homewood
Esher, see The Homewood
Essex, Wood farm, Gardener's Cottage 135
exhibition stands 53–4, 135

Fairmile Hotel, Cobham 86, 140, **146**
Fawcett, Robin and Georgina 106–7
Festival of Britain 48

INDEX

Firs, The, 24 Spaniards End, London **x**, 59–61, **61**, **62**, **63**, 136, **141**
First World War 2
Forte, Sir Charles, 48, 73, 76, 82, 83, 86, 137, 138, 139, 140
Freeman, Hardy and Willis 52, **54**, 135
French, John 102
Fry, Maxwell 12, 13

Gabor, Zsa Zsa 105
Gardner, James 48
Gibberd, Sir Frederick 121, 131n18
Gibberd, Lady (Pat) xi, 121, **122**, 131n20
Girouard, Mark 68, 70
Glenferness Avenue, Bournemouth 55, 57, **58**, 136, **141**
Gloag, John 13
GM Associates 73
Goodrich, Ontario, Canada 40
Goldfinger, Ernö ix, 35, 121
Greaves, Walter 93
Grey, John 73, 112
Griffiths, Vivien 108–9, 140
Gropius, Walter 12, 16
Grovewood, Wentworth xi, 92–3, **94**, 138, **142**
Gwynne, Colonel Alban 2
Gwynne, Commander Alban Lewis 2, **3**, 4, **9**, 16, 26, 33, 39, 40, **124**, 126n6, 136
 financial ventures 5, 13, 25
Gwynne, Revd Alban Thomas 1
Gwynne, Gladys 41
Gwynne, Mary Anne 2
Gwynne, Noreen Gwyneth

(Babs, Mrs Cruddas) 3, 4, **9**, 15, 26, 33, 39–40, 111, 121, 135
Gwynne (Alban) Patrick **xiii**, 7, **10**, **41**, **112**, **122**
 architectural apprenticeship 11–12
 architectural revelation 6, 8
 architectural style xi, xii
 archive xi
 birth 2
 cinefilms xi, xii, 40, 117
 colour theories 35, 37
 continental tour (1933) 15–16
 cooking 1, 4, 115
 death xi, 111, 123
 drawing techniques and equipment 98, 113–14
 early life 2–8
 entertaining at The Homewood 115–16, 119–20
 family background 1–2
 first commissions 21–23
 first post-war commissions 42–5
 furniture xi–xii, 13, 23, 33, 46, 60, 63, 69–70, 92–4, 11, 116–19
 homosexuality vii, viii, xii, 105
 interiors, attention to vii
 landscaping 4, 37, 92, 111, 114, 120
 motor cars 15–16, 18, 60, 66
 musical appreciation 4, 8, 50, 52, **53**, 114
 office 112–13, 122
 post-war rebuilding 41, 42

 proportion 35
 relationship with Rand 114
 reputation xi
 RIBA membership 42, 127n4
 school days 5, 6, 7, 8
 Second World War service 39–42, **41**
 staff 112–16
 war service 39–42
Gwynne, Ruby Muriel Beatrice (née Bond) 1, 2, **3**, 4, 7, 15, 25, 26, 33, 39–40, 124

Harrow School 5, 6, 7, 8
Hart Medical Surgery, Henley-on-Thames 82–3, **83**, 139, **145**
Harvey, Laurence 99, 101–5, **103**, **104**, 115, 119, 137, 139
Harvey, Domino 102
Harvey, Sophie 102
Hastings, Hubert de Cronin 13
Hawkins, Colin and Jacqui 98
Hawkins, Jack 55, 115, 136
Hawkins House 55, 57, **58**, 136, **141**
Hays Mews, Mayfair, London 106, 140
Heal's, London 62
Henley-on-Thames
 Hart Medical Surgery 82–3, **83**, 139, **145**
 Past Field, 9 Rotherfield Road 64, 66, **67**, 68, 137, **142**
Hensman, Donald 101
Heston Motor Services Area, 83, 134, **144**
High and Over, Amersham **xvi**, 8, 92

153

Hilltop house 139
Holden, Charles 6
Home 63
Homewood, Esher 2–6, **5**, 13, **14**, 15, 25
   landscape 4
Homewood, The, Esher ix, xi, xii, xv, 1, 24–37, **24**, **27**, **28**, **29**, **30**, **31**, **32**, **34**, **36**, 39, 61, 63, 66, **110**, 111–23, **112**, **116**, **118**, **119**, **120**, **122**, **124**, 126n3, 131n1, **132**, 134, 140, **141**
   architectural drawings 26, **31**, **36**
   bedroom wing **29**, 33
   bedrooms 28, 117, 122–3
   Coates's involvement 25–6, 127–8n2
   colour 35, 37, 123
   construction 26, **27**
   cost 26
   dining room 28, **31**, 33, 117, **120**
   enamelled steel panels **110**, 117, 119, 131n19, 131n21
   exterior finish 117, 119, 131n19, 131n21
   façades 28, **30**, **36**
   furniture xi–xii, 33, 111, 112, 117, 122
   Garden Cottage 114, 137, 143
   home cinema 117
   housewarming party 26
   kitchen 25, 28, **29**, 30, 116–17
   landscape 37, 111, 120, 123
   listed building status 120–1
   living room **xv**, 28, 30, **31**, **32**, 33, 117, **118**, 119, 131n18
   master dressing room **34**
   National Trust takes over xi, xii, xiii, 121–3
   ornamental pool **28**, 37, 117
   outdoor dining area 119–20
   parties 115–16
   piles 26
   plan 28
   Porte cochère **29**
   position 25
   powder room 33
   ratios 35
   sauna 119
   schedule 26
   Second World War 39–40
   servant / staff quarters 114, 119, 123
   staff 112–14, 130n10
   staircase **24**, 28, **28**, 33
   studio / office 111–12, **112**
   Studio Cottage 137, 140
   swimming pool 119
   tenants 39–40
   terrace 26, 28, 37, 121, **122**
   upgrading 116–17, **118**, 119–20, **119**, **120**, 140
   windows 30, **32**, 33, 117
Hope, Alice 59
Hornung, Mr and Mrs 64
Hotel Phoenicia 86, 138, **144**
House and Garden 48

Ideal Home and Gardening 46, 55, 57, 59, **63**, 111, **135**
Ideal Home Exhibition 25
Ionides, Alexander 5, 126n8
Isherwood, Christopher 16

Isobar, Lawn Road 16
Isokon 127n10, 133
Italy vii, 102

Jacobsen, Arne 111
Jay, Bernard 115
Jeanneret, Charles-Édouard, see Le Corbusier
Jellicoe, Sir Geoffrey 106
Jennings, Frank 11
Jones, Susannah 1

Kidderpore Avenue, no.3, London 99, 101–4, **104**, 105, 139, **143**
King, Robert (Bob) 98–9, 112, 113
Kingston upon Thames
   Bentall's department store 68, 70, 137
   Coombe Hill Road 59, **60**, 64, 136, **141**
Knapp, Stefan 77, 85, 102, **110**, 117–8, 131n19 131n21, 137
Knowles, Kenneth and Muriel 98–9, 139

Lamb, Fiona 122–3
Lasdun, Sir Denys ix, 1, 17, 18, 20, 25, **28**, 35, 37, 42, 76, 106, 115, 117, 134
Latimer, Hugh 55, 101
Lawford, Peter 101
Lawn Road Flats, London 16, 133
Le Corbusier ix, 16, 17, 28, 30, 35, 102
Lever, Jill xii
Lewenhaupt, Count Eric and Dora 16, 127n7
Lindford, Hampshire, swimming pool 140

INDEX

London 106
  Bedford Row, Holborn 52, 136
  3 Beechworth Close 64, 137, **142**
  4 Beechworth Close 61–3, **64**, **65**, 137, 142
  49 Berkeley Square 106, 140
  Blackheath 'Courtyard House' xii, 93, **95**, 114, 129n9, 130n9, 139, 141
  10 Blackheath Park **vi**, **viii**, 93, **96**, **97**, 138, **142**
  115 Blackheath Park 45–6, **45**, **46**, **47**, 134, **141**
  1–13 Blackheath Village 107–8, 140
  Bruton Street **22**, **23**, 134
  Campden Hill Road 134
  Chancery Lane 52, 136
  Coastal Chambers, Elizabeth Street 17
  Dawson Place 25, 134
  Dell Restaurant viii–ix, 76–7, **77**, **78**–**9**, 138, **144**
  EMG Handmade Gramophones, Newman Street 17, 42–3, **43**, 52, 134
  The Firs, 24 Spaniards End **x**, 59–61, **61**, **62**, **63**, 136, **141**
  Freeman, Hardy and Willis, Catford 52, **54**, 135
  Hays Mews, Mayfair 106, 140
  Hyde Park 73–9
  3 Kidderpore Avenue 99, 101–4, **104**, 105, 139, **143**

Lawn Road Flats 16, 133
London Press Exchange, 110 St Martin's Lane 53, 136
Manor Fields estate, Putney Hill 11, **12**
Mayfair Colour Centre, London 136
Mews House, Marble Arch **21**, **23**, 133
National Gallery extension 54, 107, **108**, 136, 140
Notting Hill Gate, Sweett House 50, 134
Ox on the Roof Restaurant, Chelsea 55, **57**, 135
10 Palace Gate, Kensington 10, 18, 26, 33, 127n11, 133
22 Parkgate 95–6, 98, **99**, **100**, 140, **143**
Parliamentary Offices, Bridge Street 105, 139
Royal College of Physicians ix, 17
26 St James's Place, 106, 140
Serpentine Restaurant, Hyde Park xi, 73–6, **74**, **75**, 81, 137, **144**
South Bank restaurant, Festival of Britain 48, 134
2 South Parade, Bedford Park 108–9, 140
swimming pool, Hampstead 139
4 Upper Brook Street, Mayfair 50, **51**, 127n13, 134
White House, Highgate, music studio 46, 48, **49**, 135

Whiteley's department store 35
2 Willow Road, Hampstead ix, 35, 121
18 Yeoman's Row 18, **19**, 35, 133
London Press Exchange, 110 St Martin's Lane 53, 136
London Underground 6
Lubetkin, Berthold 42, 127n3
Lutyens, Sir Edwin 11, 39–40
Lutyens, Robert 39
Lyons, Eric 45, 93, 138

McAlpine, Sir Robert 73
McGrath, Raymond 12
Malibu, California 101, 105, 139, **143**
Malta
  Hotel Phoenicia 86, 138, **144**
  Seaside House, Mellieha Bay 138
  Vista Point, St Paul's Bay 86–8, **87**, 138, **145**
Manor Fields estate, Putney Hill 11, **12**
Manser, José 63
Manser, Michael, 63, 76, 121, 140
Marie, Queen of Romania 6
Mathsson, Bruno xii, 23, 32
Mayfair Colour Centre, London 136
Mendelsohn, Erich 12–13, 16, 26
Menzies, Janet xiii, 115–16, 123
Menzies, Raymond xiii, 114–15, **116**, 120, 123
Mews House, Marble Arch, London **21**, **23**, 133

155

Mies van der Rohe, Ludwig 16, 30
Miller, Tony 112
Mineralite 61
Ministry of Public Buildings and Works 73
Mintoff, Dom 88
Modern Architectural Research Group (MARS) 17, 26, 50
Monk, Kenneth 52, 55, 59, 60, 73, 86–8, 108, 136, 138
Mountbatten, Lord 39
music rooms 46, 48, **49**, 135, 136

National Gallery extension 54, 107, **108**, 136, 140
National Trust ix, xi–xiii, 1, 63, 121–3, 140
Neel, Edric 17, 18, 20, 25, 35, 45
Nervi, Pier Luigi 83
New Ash Green, Kent 138
Notting Hill Gate, Sweett House 50, 134

oil crisis (1973) 105
Ostwald, Frederich Wilhelm 37
Ox on the Roof Restaurant, Chelsea 55, **57**, 135
Ozenfant, Amédée 35

Palace Gate, no.10, Kensington 18, 26, 33, 127n11, 133
Palladio, Andrea vii
Paris 17, 95
Parkgate, no.22, London 95–6, 98, **99**, **100**, 140, **143**
Parliamentary Offices competition 105, 139

Past Field, 9 Rotherfield Road Henley-on-Thames 64, 66, **67**, 68, 137, **142**
Pattern, Richard 112
Petersham 12
Pevsner, Sir Nikolaus 82
Picasso, Pablo 106
plan forms vii, ix, 18, 28, 30, 52, 59, 61, 64, 66, 68, 82, 84, 85, 88, 93, 95, 98, 106, 107, 119
Poelzig, Hans 16
Portchester, Hampshire 2
Potvin, John viii
Powers, Alan xi
Practical Equipment Ltd (PEL) 17
Pritchard, Jack and Molly 127n10, 133
Private Eye 108
Profumo, John 15
public work viii–ix, 73–9
Purism 35
Pyefleet apartment block, Angmering-on-Sea 108, 140

Rachlis, Michael 55
Rand, Geoffrey 66, 114, **115**, 117
ratios, use of 35
Reed, Sharon 60
Reilly, Charles 37
Richards, Oliver 112
Rigal, Annette 95
Ripley, Ryde Farm Estate 86, 139, **143**
Royal College of Physicians, London ix, 17
Royal Fine Art Commission 76
Royal Institute of British Architects xii, xiii, 42

Royal Institute of Chartered Surveyors, exhibition stand 54, 135
Ruhemann, Fritz (Frederick) 108
Ryde Farm Estate, Ripley 86, 139, **143**

Saarinen, Eero 111
Saffa Park, Dubai 84–6, **85**, 139, **146**
St James's Place, no.26, London 106, 140
St Martin's Lane, no.110, London 53, 136
St Paul-de-Vence 105, 139, **143**
St Paul's Bay, Malta, Vista Point 86–8, **87**, 138, **145**
St Tropez 105
Salmon, Dr Anthony (Tony) 59, 66, 68, 82, 114
Salmon, Elizabeth (Liz, née Humphreys) 66, 68
Samuely, Felix 26, 50
Sandroyd School, Cobham 5, 6, 55
Sargent, William 60–1
Scott, David 126n3
Scott, Sir George Gilbert 6
Second World War, 39–42, **41**
Seeger, Stanley J xiv, 105–6, 140
Serpentine Restaurant, Hyde Park, London xi, 73–6, **74**, **75**, 81, 137, **144**
Shaw, David and Jean 93, 138
Shipwrights, Benfleet 20, **20**, 28, 133
Skikne, Zvi Mosheh, see Harvey, Laurence
Soimenow, Mitrofan 12
Somake, Ellis 42

INDEX

South Bank restaurant, competition design 48, 134
South Parade, 2 Bedford Park, London 108–9, 140
Span Developments Ltd 44–5, 93, 95, 138
Spaniards End, no.24, The Firs **x**, 59–61, **61**, **62**, **63**, 136, **141**
Staircases
   3 Beechworth Close 64
   10 Blackheath Park **vi**, 93, 95
   Coombe Hill Road 59
   Grovewood 92
   Homewood 2
   The Homewood **24**, 28, **28**, 33, 37
   22 Parkgate 98
   26 St James's Place 106
   24 Spaniards End, The Firs **x**, 59–60, 63
   Vista Point, Angmering-on-Sea **ii**, 88, **92**
   Witley Park 70, **71**
   Winterdown 107
   York, Theatre Royal **80**, **81**, 82
Steele, Gary 70
Stic B 13, 16, 26, 117, 127n3
Stockholm Exhibition (1930) 6, 8
Stone, Paulene (Mrs Harvey) 102–6, **103**, 115
Stuttgart
   Schocken department store 16
   Weissenhof Estate 16
Styan, George 81–2

Supreme Radio, Edmonton 43, **44**
Sutton Place, Surrey 105–6, 140
Sweett, Cyril 26, 46, 50, 52, 134, 136
Sweett House, Notting Hill Gate 50, 52
swimming pool, Hampstead, London 139
swimming pool, Lindford, Hampshire 140

Taut, Bruno 16
Taylor, Elizabeth 101, 105
Tecton 42, 108
Theatre Royal, York ix, xi, 72, 77, **80**, **81**, 81–2, 93, 112, 115, 130–1n15, 138, **145**
Thomas, Rodney 17, 45
Thompson, Peter 63, 69, 70
Treasures in Trust (TV Programme) 121
Tugendhat House, Brno 33
Tugwell, Frank A 82

United Arab Emirates 84, 139, 140
Upper Brook Street, no.4, Mayfair 50, **51**, 127n13, 134

Vista Point, Angmering-on-Sea 88, **89**, **90–1**, 92, 108, 138, **143**
Vista Point, St Paul's Bay, Malta 86–8, **87**, 138, 145
Von Krauschen, Peter Klaus, and apartment **21**, 23, 133

Walden, Mr 66
Wallis, Gilbert and Partners 17
Warrington, Burtonwood Motorway Services Area 82–4, **84**, 129n7, 139, **146**
Weissenhof Estate, Stuttgart 16
Westwood Road, Windlesham 102, 137, **142**
Wheeler, John 17
Whitehaven civic hall competition 138
White House music studio 46, 48, **49**, 135
Winser and Newton 37
Winterdown, Portsmouth Road, Esher 106–7, **107**, 140
Witley Park, Godalming, xii, 68–70, **69**, **71**, 92, 137, **142**
Wood Farm, Essex, Gardener's Cottage 135
Wright, Lily and Bert 114, 130n10
Wyborn, John 20, 133

Yeoman's Row, no.18, London 18, **19**, 35, 133
York, Theatre Royal ix, xi, 72, 77, **80**, **81**, 81–2, 93, 112, 115, 130–1n15, 138, **145**
Yorke, F R S 12, 33